THE GLENCOE LITERATURE LIBRARY

Death Comes for the Archbishop

with Related Readings

New York, New York Columbus, Ohio Chicago, Illinois Peoria, Illinois Woodland Hills, California

Acknowledgments

Grateful acknowledgment is given authors, publishers, photographers, museums, and agents for permission to reprint the following copyrighted material. Every effort has been made to determine copyright owners. In case of any omissions, the Publisher will be pleased to make suitable acknowledgments in future editions.

Copyright © 1927, 1929 by Willa Cather. Copyright renewed 1955, 1957 by the Executors of the Estate of Willa Cather. Reprinted by arrangement with Alfred A. Knopf, a division of Random House, Inc.

From *Willa Cather on Writing* by Willa Cather, copyright © 1949 by the Executors of the Estate of Willa Cather. Used by permission of Alfred A. Knopf, a division of Random House, Inc.

"Through Tewa Eyes" by Alfonso Ortiz. *National Geographic*, October 1991. Reprinted by permission of the National Geographic Society.

"In 1864" by Luci Tapahonso. Reprinted by permission of the author.

"Where Mountain Lion Lay Down with Deer," copyright © 1981 by Leslie Marmon Silko, reprinted with the permission of The Wylie Agency, Inc.

"American Odyssey: Cycling the Santa Fe Trail" by Dennis L. Coello. *Bicycling*, September/October 1982. Reprinted by permission of Rodale Press.

Cover Art: *Purple Bluff*, Frank Reed Whiteside (1866–1929); David David Gallery, Philadelphia/Superstock.

Glencoe/McGraw-Hill
*A Division of The **McGraw·Hill** Companies*

Copyright ©2002 The McGraw-Hill Companies, Inc. All rights reserved. Except as permitted under the United States Copyright Act of 1976, no part of this publication may be reproduced or distributed in any form or by any means, or stored in a database or retrieval system, without prior written permission of the publisher.

Send all inquiries to:
Glencoe/McGraw-Hill
8787 Orion Place
Columbus, OH 43240

ISBN 0-07-826102-3
Printed in the United States of America
1 2 3 4 5 6 7 8 9 026 04 03 02

Contents

Death Comes for the Archbishop

Prologue	At Rome	1
Book One	The Vicar Apostolic	9
Book Two	Missionary Journeys	29
Book Three	The Mass at Ácoma	45
Book Four	Snake Root	65
Book Five	Padre Martínez	77
Book Six	Doña Isabella	97
Book Seven	The Great Diocese	111
Book Eight	Gold Under Pike's Peak	133
Book Nine	Death Comes for the Archbishop	147

Continued

Contents *Continued*

Related Readings   **169**

Willa Cather	**On *Death Comes for the Archbishop***	letter to the editor	**171**
Alfonso Ortiz	**Through Tewa Eyes: Origins**	magazine article	**176**
Luci Tapahonso	**In 1864**	poem	**182**
John Donne	**Holy Sonnet 167**	poem	**186**
Leslie Marmon Silko	**Where Mountain Lion Lay Down with Deer**	poem	**187**
Dennis L. Coello	**American Odyssey: Cycling the Santa Fe Trail**	magazine article	**189**

Death Comes for the Archbishop

Willa Cather

PROLOGUE

At Rome

One summer evening in the year 1848, three Cardinals and a missionary Bishop from America were dining together in the gardens of a villa in the Sabine hills, overlooking Rome. The villa was famous for the fine view from its terrace. The hidden garden in which the four men sat at table lay some twenty feet below the south end of this terrace, and was a mere shelf of rock, overhanging a steep declivity planted with vineyards. A flight of stone steps connected it with the promenade above. The table stood in a sanded square, among potted orange and oleander trees, shaded by spreading ilex oaks that grew out of the rocks overhead. Beyond the balustrade was the drop into the air, and far below the landscape stretched soft and undulating; there was nothing to arrest the eye until it reached Rome itself.

It was early when the Spanish Cardinal and his guests sat down to dinner. The sun was still good for an hour of supreme splendour, and across the shining folds of country the low profile of the city barely fretted the skyline—indistinct except for the dome of St. Peter's, bluish grey like the flattened top of a great balloon, just a flash of copper light on its soft metallic surface. The Cardinal had an eccentric preference for beginning his dinner at this time in the late afternoon, when the vehemence of the sun suggested motion. The light was full of action and had a peculiar quality of climax—of splendid finish. It was both intense and soft, with a ruddiness as of much-multiplied candlelight, an aura of red in its flames. It bored into the ilex trees, illuminating their mahogany trunks and blurring their dark foliage; it warmed the bright green of the orange trees and the rose of the oleander blooms to gold; sent congested spiral patterns quivering over the damask and plate and crystal. The churchmen kept their rectangular clerical caps on their heads to protect them from the sun. The three Cardinals wore black cassocks with crimson pipings and crimson buttons, the Bishop a long black coat over his violet vest.

They were talking business; had met, indeed, to discuss an anticipated appeal from the Provincial Council at Baltimore for the founding of an Apostolic Vicarate in New Mexico—a part of North America recently annexed to the United States. This new territory was vague to all of them, even to the missionary Bishop. The Italian and French Cardinals spoke of it as *Le Mexique,* and the Spanish host referred to it as "New Spain."

Their interest in the projected Vicarate was tepid, and had to be continually revived by the missionary, Father Ferrand; Irish by birth, French by ancestry —a man of wide wanderings and notable achievement in the New World, an Odysseus of the Church. The language spoken was French—the time had already gone by when Cardinals could conveniently discuss contemporary matters in Latin.

The French and Italian Cardinals were men in vigorous middle life—the Norman full-belted and ruddy, the Venetian spare and sallow and hook-nosed. Their host, García María de Allande, was still a young man. He was dark in colouring, but the long Spanish face, that looked out from so many canvases in his ancestral portrait gallery, was in the young Cardinal much modified through his English mother. With his *caffè oscuro* eyes, he had a fresh, pleasant English mouth, and an open manner.

During the latter years of the reign of Gregory XVI, de Allende had been the most influential man at the Vatican; but since the death of Gregory, two years ago, he had retired to his country estate. He believed the reforms of the new Pontiff impractical and dangerous, and had withdrawn from politics, confining his activities to work for the Society for the Propagation of the Faith—that organization which had been so fostered by Gregory. In his leisure the Cardinal played tennis. As a boy, in England, he had been passionately fond of this sport. Lawn tennis had not yet come into fashion; it was a formidable game of indoor tennis the Cardinal played. Amateurs of that violent sport came from Spain and France to try their skill against him.

The missionary, Bishop Ferrand, looked much older than any of them, old and rough—except for his clear, intensely blue eyes. His diocese lay within the icy arms of the Great Lakes, and on his long, lonely horseback rides among his missions the sharp winds had bitten him well. The missionary was here for a purpose, and he pressed his point. He ate more rapidly than the others and had plenty of time to plead his cause,—finished each course with such dispatch that the Frenchman remarked he would have been an ideal dinner companion for Napoleon.

The Bishop laughed and threw out his brown hands in apology. "Likely enough I have forgot my manners. I am preoccupied. Here you can scarcely understand what it means that the United States has annexed that enormous territory which was the cradle of the Faith in the New World. The Vicarate of New Mexico will be in a few years raised to an Episcopal See, with jurisdiction over a country larger than Central and Western Europe, barring Russia. The Bishop of that See will direct the beginning of momentous things."

"Beginnings," murmured the Venetian, "there have been so many. But nothing ever comes from over there but trouble and appeals for money."

The missionary turned to him patiently. "Your Eminence, I beg you to follow me. This country was evangelized in fifteen hundred, by the Franciscan Fathers. It has been allowed to drift for nearly three hundred years and is not yet dead. It still pitifully calls itself a Catholic country, and tries to keep the forms of religion without instruction. The old mission churches are in ruins. The few priests are without guidance or discipline. They are lax in religious observance, and some of them live in open concubinage. If this Augean stable is not cleansed, now that the territory has been taken over by a progressive government, it will prejudice the interests of the Church in the whole of North America."

"But these missions are still under the jurisdiction of Mexico, are they not?" inquired the Frenchman.

"In the See of the Bishop of Durango?" added María de Allande.

The missionary sighed. "Your Eminence, the Bishop of Durango is an old man; and from his seat to Sante Fé is a distance of fifteen hundred English miles. There are no wagon roads, no canals, no navigable rivers. Trade is carried on by means of pack-mules, over treacherous trails. The desert down there has a peculiar horror; I do not mean thirst, nor Indian massacres, which are frequent. The very floor of the world is cracked open into countless canyons and arroyos, fissures in the earth which are sometimes ten feet deep, sometimes a thousand. Up and down these stony chasms the traveller and his mules clamber as best they can. It is impossible to go far in any direction without crossing them. If the Bishop of Durango should summon a disobedient priest by letter, who shall bring the Padre to him? Who can prove that he ever received the summons? The post is carried by hunters, fur trappers, gold seekers, whoever happens to be moving on the trails."

The Norman Cardinal emptied his glass and wiped his lips.

"And the inhabitants, Father Ferrand? If these are the travellers, who stays at home?"

"Some thirty Indian nations, Monsignor, each with its own customs and language, many of them fiercely hostile to each other. And the Mexicans, a naturally devout people. Untaught and unshepherded, they cling to the faith of their fathers."

"I have a letter from the Bishop of Durango, recommending his Vicar for this new post," remarked María de Allande.

"Your Eminence, it would be a great misfortune if a native priest were appointed; they have never done well in that field. Besides, this Vicar is old. The new Vicar must be a young man, of strong constitution, full of zeal, and above all, intelligent. He will have to deal with savagery and ignorance, with dissolute priests and political intrigue. He must be a man to whom order is necessary—as dear as life."

The Spaniard's coffee-coloured eyes showed a glint of yellow as he glanced sidewise at his guest. "I suspect, from your exordium, that you have a candidate—and that he is a French priest, perhaps?"

"You guess rightly, Monsignor. I am glad to see that we have the same opinion of French missionaries."

"Yes," said the Cardinal lightly, "they are the best missionaries. Our Spanish fathers made good martyrs, but the French Jesuits accomplish more. They are the great organizers."

"Better than the Germans?" asked the Venetian, who had Austrian sympathies.

"Oh, the Germans classify, but the French arrange! The French missionaries have a sense of proportion and rational adjustment. They are always trying to discover the logical relation of things. It is a passion with them." Here the host turned to the old Bishop again. "But your Grace, why do you neglect this Burgundy? I had this wine brought up from my cellar especially to warm away the chill of your twenty Canadian winters. Surely, you do not gather vintages like this on the shores of the Great Lake Huron?"

The missionary smiled as he took up his untouched glass. "It is superb, your Eminence, but I fear I have lost my palate for vintages. Out there, a little whisky, or Hudson Bay Company rum, does better for us. I must confess I enjoyed the champagne in Paris. We had been forty days at sea, and I am a poor sailor."

"Then we must have some for you." He made a sign to his major-domo. "You like it very cold? And your new Vicar Apostolic, what will he drink in the country of bison and *serpents à sonnettes?* And what will he eat?"

"He will eat dried buffalo meat and frijoles with chili, and he will be glad to drink water when he can get it. He will have no easy life, your Eminence. That country will drink up his youth and strength as it does the rain. He will be called upon for every sacrifice, quite possibly for martyrdom. Only last year the Indian pueblo of San Fernandez de Taos murdered and scalped the American Governor and some dozen other whites. The reason they did not scalp their Padre, was that their Padre was one of the leaders of the rebellion and himself planned the massacre. That is how things stand in New Mexico!"

"Where is your candidate at present, Father?"

"He is a parish priest, on the shores of Lake Ontario, in my diocese. I have watched his work for nine years. He is but thirty-five now. He came to us directly from the Seminary."

"And his name is?"

"Jean Marie Latour."

María de Allande, leaning back in his chair put the tips of his long fingers together and regarded them thoughtfully.

"Of course, Father Ferrand, the Propaganda will almost certainly appoint to this Vicarate the man whom the council at Baltimore recommends."

"Ah yes, your Eminence; but a word from you to the Provincial Council, an inquiry, a suggestion——"

"Would have some weight, I admit," replied the Cardinal smiling. "And this Latour is intelligent, you say? What a fate you are drawing upon him! But I suppose it is no worse than a life among the Hurons. My knowledge of your country is chiefly drawn from the romances of Fenimore Cooper, which I read in English with great pleasure. But has your priest a versatile intelligence? Any intelligence in matters of art, for example?"

"And what need would he have for that, Monsignor? Besides, he is from Auvergne."

The three Cardinals broke into laughter and refilled their glasses. They were all becoming restive under the monotonous persistence of the missionary.

"Listen," said the host, "and I will relate a little story, while the Bishop does me the compliment to drink my champagne. I have a reason for asking this question which you have answered so finally. In my family house in Valencia I have a number of pictures by the great Spanish painters, collected chiefly by my great-grandfather, who was a man of perception in these things and, for his time, rich. His collection of El Greco is, I believe, quite the best in Spain. When my progenitor was an old man, along came one of these missionary priests from New Spain, begging. All missionaries from the Americas were inveterate beggars, then as now, Bishop Ferrand. This Franciscan had considerable success, with his tales of pious Indian converts and struggling missions. He came to visit at my great-grandfather's house and conducted devotions in the absence of the Chaplain. He wheedled a good sum of money out of the old man, as well as vestments and linen and chalices—he would take anything—and he implored my grandfather to give him a painting from his great collection, for the ornamentation of his mission church among the Indians. My grandfather told him to choose from the gallery, believing the priest would covet most what he himself could best afford to spare. But not at all; the hairy Franciscan pounced upon one of the best in the collection; a young St. Francis in meditation, by El Greco, and the model for the saint was one of the very handsome Dukes of Albuquerque. My grandfather protested; tried to persuade the fellow that some picture of the Crucifixion, or a martyrdom, would appeal more strongly to his redskins. What would a St. Francis, of almost feminine beauty, mean to the scalp-takers?

"All in vain. The missionary turned upon his host with a reply which has become a saying in our family: 'You refuse me this picture because it is a good picture. *It is too good for God, but it is not too good for you.*'

"He carried off the painting. In my grandfather's manuscript catalogue, under the number and title of the St. Francis, is written: *Given to Fray Teodocio, for the glory of God, to enrich his mission church at Pueblo de Cia, among the savages of New Spain.*

"It is because of this lost treasure, Father Ferrand, that I happened to have had some personal correspondence with the Bishop of Durango. I once wrote the facts to him fully. He replied to me that the mission at Cia was long ago destroyed and its furnishings scattered. Of course the painting may have been ruined in a pillage or massacre. On the other hand, it may still be hidden away in some crumbling sacristy or smoky wigwam. If your French priest had a discerning eye, now, and were sent to this Vicarate, he might keep my El Greco in mind."

The Bishop shook his head. "No, I can't promise you—I do not know. I have noticed that he is a man of severe and refined tastes, but he is very reserved. Down there the Indians do not dwell in wigwams, your Eminence," he added gently.

"No matter, Father. I see your redskins through Fenimore Cooper, and I like them so. Now let us go to the terrace for our coffee and watch the evening come on."

The Cardinal led his guests up the narrow stairway. The long gravelled terrace and its balustrade were blue as a lake in the dusky air. Both sun and shadows were gone. The folds of russet country were now violet. Waves of rose and gold throbbed up the sky from behind the dome of the Basilica.

As the churchmen walked up and down the promenade, watching the stars come out, their talk touched upon many matters, but they avoided politics, as men are apt to do in dangerous times. Not a word was spoken of the Lombard war, in which the Pope's position was so anomalous. They talked instead of a new opera by young Verdi, which was being sung in Venice; of the case of a Spanish dancing-girl who had lately become a religious and was said to be working miracles in Andalusia. In this conversation the missionary took no part, nor could he even follow it with much interest. He asked himself whether he had been on the frontier so long that he had quite lost his taste for the talk of clever men. But before they separated for the night María de Allande spoke a word in his ear, in English.

"You are *distrait*, Father Ferrand. Are you wishing to unmake your new Bishop already? It is too late. Jean Marie Latour—am I right?"

DEATH COMES FOR THE ARCHBISHOP

BOOK ONE

The Vicar Apostolic

1
The Cruciform Tree

One afternoon in the autumn of 1851 a solitary horseman, followed by a pack-mule, was pushing through an arid stretch of country somewhere in central New Mexico. He had lost his way, and was trying to get back to the trail, with only his compass and his sense of direction for guides. The difficulty was that the country in which he found himself was so featureless—or rather, that it was crowded with features, all exactly alike. As far as he could see, on every side, the landscape was heaped up into monotonous red sand-hills, not much larger than haycocks, and very much the shape of haycocks. One could not have believed that in the number of square miles a man is able to sweep with the eye there could be so many uniform red hills. He had been riding among them since early morning, and the look of the country had no more changed than if he had stood still. He must have travelled through thirty miles of these conical red hills, winding his way in the narrow cracks between them, and he had begun to think that he would never see anything else. They were so exactly like one another that he seemed to be wandering in some geometrical nightmare; flattened cones, they were, more the shape of Mexican ovens than haycocks—yes, exactly the shape of Mexican ovens, red as brick-dust, and naked of vegetation except for small juniper trees. And the junipers, too, were the shape of Mexican ovens. Every conical hill was spotted with smaller cones of juniper, a uniform yellowish green, as the hills were a uniform red. The hills thrust out of the ground so thickly that they seemed to be pushing each other, elbowing each other aside, tipping each other over.

The blunted pyramid, repeated so many hundred times upon his retina and crowding down upon him in the heat, had confused the traveller, who was sensitive to the shape of things.

"*Mais, c'est fantastique!*" he muttered, closing his eyes to rest them from the intrusive omnipresence of the triangle.

When he opened his eyes again, his glance immediately fell upon one juniper which differed in shape from the others. It was not a thick-growing cone, but a naked, twisted trunk, perhaps ten feet high, and at the top it parted into two lateral, flat-lying branches, with a little crest of green in the centre, just above the cleavage. Living vegetation could not present more faithfully the form of the Cross.

The traveller dismounted, drew from his pocket a much worn book, and baring his head, knelt at the foot of the cruciform tree.

Under his buckskin riding-coat he wore a black vest and the cravat and collar of a churchman. A young priest, at his devotions; and a priest in a thousand, one knew at a glance. His bowed head was not that of an ordinary man,—it was built for the seat of a fine intelligence. His brow was open, generous, reflective, his features handsome and somewhat severe. There was a singular elegance about the hands below the fringed cuffs of the buckskin jacket. Everything showed him to be a man of gentle birth—brave, sensitive, courteous. His manners, even when he was alone in the desert, were distinguished. He had a kind of courtesy toward himself, toward his beasts, toward the juniper tree before which he knelt, and the God whom he was addressing.

His devotions lasted perhaps half an hour, and when he rose he looked refreshed. He began talking to his mare in halting Spanish, asking whether she agreed with him that it would be better to push on, weary as she was, in hope of finding the trail. He had no water left in his canteen, and the horses had had none since yesterday morning. They had made a dry camp in these hills last night. The animals were almost at the end of their endurance, but they would not recuperate until they got water, and it seemed best to spend their last strength in searching for it.

On a long caravan trip across Texas this man had had some experience of thirst, as the party with which he travelled was several times put on a meagre water ration for days together. But he had not suffered then as he did now. Since morning he had had a feeling of illness; the taste of fever in his mouth, and alarming seizures of vertigo. As these conical hills pressed closer and closer upon him, he began to wonder whether his long wayfaring from the mountains of Auvergne were possibly to end here. He reminded himself of that cry, wrung from his Saviour on the Cross, "*J'ai soif!*" Of all our Lord's physical sufferings, only one, "I thirst," rose to His lips. Empowered by long training, the young priest blotted himself out of his own consciousness and meditated upon the anguish of his Lord. The Passion of Jesus became for him the only reality; the need of his own body was but a part of that conception.

His mare stumbled, breaking his mood of contemplation. He was sorrier for his beasts than for himself. He, supposed to be the intelligence of the party, had got the poor animals into this interminable desert of ovens. He was afraid he had been absent-minded, had been pondering his problem instead of heeding the way. His problem was how to recover a Bishopric. He was a Vicar Apostolic, lacking a Vicarate. He was thrust out; his flock would have none of him.

The traveller was Jean Marie Latour, consecrated Vicar Apostolic of New Mexico and Bishop of Agathonica *in partibus* at Cincinnati a year ago—and ever since then he had been trying to reach his Vicarate. No one in Cincinnati could tell him how to get to New Mexico—no one had ever been there. Since young Father Latour's arrival in America, a railroad had been built through from New York to Cincinnati; but there it ended. New Mexico lay in the middle of a dark continent. The Ohio merchants knew of two routes only. One was the Santa Fé trail from St. Louis, but at that time it was very dangerous because of Comanche Indian raids. His friends advised Father Latour to go down the river to New Orleans, thence by boat to Galveston, across Texas to San Antonio, and to wind up into New Mexico along the Rio Grande valley. This he had done, but with what misadventures!

His steamer was wrecked and sunk in the Galveston harbour, and he had lost all his worldly possessions except his books, which he saved at the risk of his life. He crossed Texas with a traders' caravan, and approaching San Antonio he was hurt in jumping from an overturning wagon, and had to lie for three months in the crowded house of a poor Irish family, waiting for his injured leg to get strong.

It was nearly a year after he had embarked upon the Mississippi that the young Bishop, at about the sunset hour of a summer afternoon, at last beheld the old settlement toward which he had been journeying so long: The wagon train had been going all day through a greasewood plain, when late in the afternoon the teamsters began shouting that over yonder was the Villa. Across the level, Father Latour could distinguish low brown shapes, like earthworks, lying at the base of wrinkled green mountains with bare tops,—wave-like mountains, resembling billows beaten up from a flat sea by a heavy gale; and their green was of two colours—aspen and evergreen, not intermingled but lying in solid areas of light and dark.

As the wagons went forward and the sun sank lower, a sweep of red carnelian-coloured hills lying at the foot of the mountains came into view; they curved like two arms about a depression in the plain; and in that depression was Santa Fé, at last! A thin, wavering adobe town . . . a green plaza . . . at one end a church with two earthen towers that rose high above the flatness. The long main street began at the church, the town seemed to flow from it like a stream from a spring. The church towers, and all the low adobe houses, were rose colour in that light,—a little darker in tone than the amphitheatre of red hills behind; and periodically the plumes of poplars flashed like gracious accent marks,—inclining and recovering themselves in the wind.

The young Bishop was not alone in the exaltation of that hour; beside him rode Father Joseph Vaillant, his boyhood friend, who had made this long pilgrimage with him and shared his dangers. The two rode into Santa Fé together, claiming it for the glory of God.

How, then, had Father Latour come to be here in the sand-hills, many miles from his seat, unattended, far out of his way and with no knowledge of how to get back to it?

On his arrival at Santa Fé, this was what had happened: the Mexican priests there had refused to recognize his authority. They disclaimed any knowledge of a Vicarate Apostolic, or a Bishop of Agathonica. They said they were under the jurisdiction of the Bishop of Durango, and had received no instructions to the contrary. If Father Latour was to be their Bishop, where were his credentials? A parchment and letters, he knew, had been sent to the Bishop of Durango, but these had evidently got no farther. There was no postal service in this part of the world; the quickest and surest way to communicate with the Bishop of Durango was to go to him. So, having travelled for nearly a year to reach Santa Fé, Father Latour left it after a few weeks, and set off alone on horseback to ride down into Old Mexico and back, a journey of a full three thousand miles.

He had been warned that there were many trails leading off the Rio Grande road, and that a stranger might easily mistake his way. For the first few days he had been cautious and watchful. Then he must have grown careless and turned into some purely local trail. When he realized that he was astray, his canteen was already empty and his horses seemed too exhausted to retrace their steps. He had persevered in this sandy track, which grew ever fainter, reasoning that it must lead somewhere.

All at once Father Latour thought he felt a change in the body of his mare. She lifted her head for the first time in a long while, and seemed to redistribute her weight upon her legs. The pack-mule behaved in a similar manner, and both quickened their pace. Was it possible they scented water?

Nearly an hour went by, and then, winding between two hills that were like all the hundreds they had passed, the two beasts whinnied simultaneously. Below them, in the midst of that wavy ocean of sand, was a green thread of verdure and a running stream. This ribbon in the desert seemed no wider than a man could throw a stone,—and it was greener than anything Latour had ever seen, even in his own greenest corner of the Old World. But for the quivering of the hide on his mare's neck and shoulders, he might have thought this a vision, a delusion of thirst.

Running water, clover fields, cottonwoods, acacias, little adobe houses with brilliant gardens, a boy driving a flock of white goats toward the stream,—that was what the young Bishop saw.

A few moments later, when he was struggling with his horses, trying to keep them from overdrinking, a young girl with a black shawl over her head came running toward him. He thought he had never seen a kindlier face. Her greeting was that of a Christian.

"Ave María Purísima, Señor. Whence do you come?"

"Blessed child," he replied in Spanish, "I am a priest who has lost his way. I am famished for water."

"A priest?" she cried, "that is not possible! Yet I look at you, and it is true. Such a thing has never happened to us before; it must be in answer to my father's prayers. Run, Pedro, and tell father and Salvatore."

2
Hidden Water

An hour later, as darkness came over the sand-hills, the young Bishop was seated at supper in the motherhouse of this Mexican settlement—which, he learned, was appropriately called *Agua Secreta,* Hidden Water. At the table with him were his host, an old man called Benito, the oldest son, and two grandsons. The old man was a widower, and his daughter, Josepha, the girl who had run to meet the Bishop at the stream, was his housekeeper. Their supper was a pot of frijoles cooked with meat, bread and goat's milk, fresh cheese and ripe apples.

From the moment he entered this room with its thick whitewashed adobe walls, Father Latour had felt a kind of peace about it. In its bareness and simplicity there was something comely, as there was about the serious girl who had placed their food before them and who now stood in the shadows against the wall, her eager eyes fixed upon his face. He found himself very much at home with the four dark-headed men who sat beside him in the candlelight. Their manners were gentle, their voices low and agreeable. When he said grace before meat, the men had knelt on the floor beside the table. The grandfather declared that the Blessed Virgin must have led the Bishop from his path and brought him here to baptize the children and to sanctify the marriages. Their settlement was little known, he said. They had no papers for their land and were afraid the Americans might take it away from them. There was no one in their settlement who could read or write. Salvatore, his oldest son, had gone all the way to Albuquerque to find a wife, and had married there. But the priest had charged him twenty pesos, and that was half of all he had saved to buy furniture and glass windows for his house. His brothers and cousins discouraged by his experience, had taken wives without the marriage sacrament.

In answer to the Bishop's questions, they told him the simple story of their lives. They had here all they needed to make them happy. They spun and wove from the fleece of their flocks, raised their own corn and wheat and tobacco, dried their plums and apricots for winter. Once a year the boys took the grain up to Albuquerque to have it ground, and bought such luxuries as sugar and coffee. They had bees, and when sugar was high they sweetened with honey. Benito did not know in what year his grandfather had settled here, coming from Chihuahua with all his goods in ox-carts. "But it was soon after the time when the French killed their king. My grandfather had heard talk of that before he left home, and used to tell us boys about it when he was an old man."

"Perhaps you have guessed that I am a Frenchman," said Father Latour.

No, they had not, but they felt sure he was not an American. José, the elder grandson, had been watching the visitor uncertainly. He was a handsome boy, with a triangle of black hair hanging over his rather sullen eyes. He now spoke for the first time.

"They say at Albuquerque that now we are all Americans, but that is not true, Padre. I will never be an American. They are infidels."

"Not all, my son. I have lived among Americans in the north for ten years, and I found many devout Catholics."

The young man shook his head. "They destroyed our churches when they were fighting us, and stabled their horses in them. And now they will take our religion away from us. We want our own ways and our own religion."

Father Latour began to tell them about his friendly relations with Protestants in Ohio, but they had not room in their minds for two ideas; there was one Church, and the rest of the world was infidel. One thing they could understand; that he had here in his saddle-bags his vestments, the altar stone, and all the equipment for celebrating the Mass; and that to-morrow morning, after Mass, he would hear confessions, baptize, and sanctify marriages.

After supper Father Latour took up a candle and began to examine the holy images on the shelf over the fireplace. The wooden figures of the saints, found in even the poorest Mexican houses, always interested him. He had never yet seen two alike. These over Benito's fireplace had come in the ox-carts from Chihuahua nearly sixty years ago. They had been carved by some devout soul, and brightly painted, though the colours had softened with time, and they were dressed in cloth, like dolls. They were much more to his taste than the factory-made plaster images in his mission churches in Ohio—more like the homely stone carvings on the front of old parish churches in Auvergne. The wooden Virgin was a sorrowing mother indeed,—long and stiff and severe, very long from the neck to the waist, even longer from waist to feet, like some of the rigid mosaics of the Eastern Church. She was dressed in black, with a white apron, and a black reboso over her head, like a Mexican woman of the poor. At her right was St. Joseph, and at her left a fierce little equestrian figure, a saint wearing the costume of a Mexican *ranchero*, velvet trousers richly embroidered and wide at the ankle, velvet jacket and silk shirt, and a high-crowned, broad-brimmed Mexican sombrero. He was attached to his fat horse by a wooden pivot driven through the saddle.

The younger grandson saw the priest's interest in this figure. "That," he said, "is my name saint, Santiago."

"Oh, yes; Santiago. He was a missionary, like me. In our country we call him St. Jacques, and he carries a staff and a wallet—but here he would need a horse, surely."

The boy looked at him in surprise. "But he is the saint of horses. Isn't he that in your country?"

The Bishop shook his head. "No. I know nothing about that. How is he the saint of horses?"

"He blesses the mares and makes them fruitful. Even the Indians believe that. They know that if they neglect to pray to Santiago for a few years, the foals do not come right."

A little later, after his devotions, the young Bishop lay down in Benito's deep feather-bed, thinking how different was this night from his anticipation of it. He had expected to make a dry camp in the wilderness, and to sleep under a juniper tree, like the Prophet, tormented by thirst. But here he lay in comfort and safety, with love for his fellow creatures flowing like peace about his heart. If Father Vaillant were here, he would say, "A miracle"; that the Holy Mother, to whom he had addressed himself before the cruciform tree, had led him hither. And it was a miracle, Father Latour knew that. But his dear Joseph must always have the miracle very direct and spectacular, not with Nature, but against it. He would almost be able to tell the colour of the mantle Our Lady wore when She took the mare by the bridle back yonder among the junipers and led her out of the pathless sand-hills, as the angel led the ass on the Flight into Egypt.

I n the late afternoon of the following day the Bishop was walking alone along the banks of the life-giving stream, reviewing in his mind the events of the morning. Benito and his daughter had made an altar before the sorrowful wooden Virgin, and placed upon it candles and flowers. Every soul in the village, except Salvatore's sick wife, had come to the Mass. He had performed marriages and baptisms and heard confessions and confirmed until noon. Then came the christening feast. José had killed a kid the night before, and immediately after her confirmation Josepha slipped away to help her sisters-in-law roast it. When Father Latour asked her to give him his portion without chili, the girl inquired whether it was more pious to eat it like that. He hastened to explain that Frenchmen, as a rule, do not like high seasoning, lest she should hereafter deprive herself of her favourite condiment.

After the feast the sleepy children were taken home, the men gathered in the plaza to smoke under the great cottonwood trees. The Bishop, feeling a need of solitude, had gone forth to walk, firmly refusing an escort. On his way he passed the earthen thrashing-floor, where these people beat out their grain and winnowed it in the wind, like the Children of Israel. He heard a frantic bleating behind him, and was overtaken by Pedro with the great flock of goats, indignant at their day's confinement, and wild to be in the fringe of pasture along the hills. They leaped the stream like arrows speeding from the bow, and regarded the Bishop as they passed him with their mocking, humanly intelligent smile. The young bucks were light and elegant in figure, with their pointed chins and polished tilted horns. There was great variety in their faces, but in nearly all something supercilious and sardonic. The angoras had long silky hair of a dazzling whiteness. As they leaped through the sunlight they brought to mind the chapter in the Apocalypse, about the whiteness of them that were washed in the blood of the Lamb. The young Bishop smiled at his mixed theology. But though the goat had always been the symbol of pagan lewdness, he told himself that their fleece had warmed many a good Christian, and their rich milk nourished sickly children.

About a mile above the village he came upon the waterhead, a spring overhung by the sharp-leafed variety of cottonwood called water willow. All about it crowded the oven-shaped hills,—nothing to hint of water until it rose miraculously out of the parched and thirsty sea of sand. Some subterranean stream found an outlet here, was released from darkness. The result was grass and trees and flowers and human life; household order and hearths from which the smoke of burning piñon logs rose like incense to Heaven.

The Bishop sat a long time by the spring, while the declining sun poured its beautifying light over those low, rose-tinted houses and bright gardens. The old grandfather had shown him arrow-heads and corroded medals, and a sword hilt, evidently Spanish, that he had found in the earth near the water-head. This spot had been a refuge for humanity long before these Mexicans had come upon it. It was older than history, like those well-heads in his own country where the Roman settlers had set up the image of a river goddess, and later the Christian priests had planted a cross. This settlement was his Bishopric in miniature; hundreds of square miles of thirsty desert, then a spring, a village, old men trying to remember their catechism to teach their grandchildren. The Faith planted by the Spanish friars and watered with their blood was not dead; it awaited only the toil of the husbandman. He was not troubled about the revolt in Santa Fé, or the powerful old native priest who led it—Father Martínez, of Taos, who had ridden over from his parish expressly to receive the new Vicar and to drive him away. He was rather terrifying, that old priest, with his big head, violent Spanish face, and shoulders like a buffalo; but the day of his tyranny was almost over.

3
The Bishop Chez Lui

It was the late afternoon of Christmas Day, and the Bishop sat at his desk writing letters. Since his return to Santa Fé his official correspondence had been heavy; but the closely-written sheets over which he bent with a thoughtful smile were not to go to Monsignori, or to Archbishops, or to the heads of religious houses,—but to France, to Auvergne, to his own little town; to a certain grey, winding street, paved with cobbles and shaded by tall chestnuts on which, even to-day, some few brown leaves would be clinging, or dropping one by one, to be caught in the cold green ivy on the walls.

The Bishop had returned from his long horseback trip into Mexico only nine days ago. At Durango the old Mexican prelate there had, after some delay, delivered to him the documents that defined his Vicarate, and Father Latour rode back the fifteen hundred miles to Santa Fé through the sunny days of early winter. On his arrival he found amity instead of enmity awaiting him. Father Vaillant had already endeared himself to the people. The Mexican priest who was in charge of the pro-cathedral had gracefully retired—gone to visit his family in Old Mexico, and carried his effects along with him. Father Vaillant had taken possession of the priest's house, and with the help of carpenters and the Mexican women of the parish had put it in order. The Yankee traders and the military Commandant at Fort Marcy had sent generous contributions of bedding and blankets and odd pieces of furniture.

The Episcopal residence was an old adobe house, much out of repair, but with possibilities of comfort. Father Latour had chosen for his study a room at one end of the wing. There he sat, as this afternoon of Christmas Day faded into evening. It was a long room of an agreeable shape. The thick clay walls had been finished on the inside by the deft palms of Indian women, and had that irregular and intimate quality of things made entirely by the human hand. There was a reassuring solidity and depth about those walls, rounded at door-sills and window-sills, rounded in wide wings about the corner fire-place. The interior had been newly whitewashed in the Bishop's absence, and the flicker of the fire threw a rosy glow over the wavy surfaces, never quite evenly flat, never a dead white, for the ruddy colour of the clay underneath gave a warm tone to the lime wash. The ceiling was made of heavy cedar beams, overlaid by aspen saplings, all of one size, lying close together like the ribs in corduroy and clad in their ruddy inner skins. The earth floor was covered with thick Indian blankets; two blankets, very old, and beautiful in design and colour, were hung on the walls like tapestries.

On either side of the fire-place, plastered recesses were let into the wall. In one, narrow and arched, stood the Bishop's crucifix. The other was square, with a carved wooden door, like a grill, and within it lay a few rare and beautiful books. The rest of the Bishop's library was on open shelves at one end of the room.

The furniture of the house Father Vaillant had bought from the departed Mexican priest. It was heavy and somewhat clumsy, but not unsightly. All the wood used in making tables and bedsteads was hewn from tree boles with the ax or hatchet. Even the thick planks on which the Bishop's theological books rested were ax-dressed. There was not at that time a turning-lathe or a saw-mill in all northern New Mexico. The native carpenters whittled out chair rungs and table legs, and fitted them together with wooden pins instead of iron nails. Wooden chests were used in place of dressers with drawers, and sometimes these were beautifully carved, or covered with decorated leather. The desk at which the Bishop sat writing was an importation, a walnut "secretary" of American make (sent down by one of the officers of the Fort at Father Vaillant's suggestion). His silver candlesticks he had brought from France long ago. They were given to him by a beloved aunt when he was ordained.

The young Bishop's pen flew over the paper, leaving a trail of fine, finished French script behind, in violet ink.

"My new study, dear brother, as I write, is full of the delicious fragrance of the piñon logs burning in my fireplace. (We use this kind of cedar-wood altogether for fuel, and it is highly aromatic, yet delicate. At our meanest tasks we have a perpetual odour of incense about us.) I wish that you, and my dear sister, could look in upon this scene of comfort and peace. We missionaries wear a frock-coat and wide-brimmed hat all day, you know, and look like American traders. What a pleasure to come home at night and put on my old cassock! I feel more like a priest then—for so much of the day I must be a 'business man'!—and, for some reason, more like a Frenchman. All day I am an American in speech and thought—yes, in heart, too. The kindness of the American traders, and especially of the military officers at the Fort, commands more than a superficial loyalty. I mean to help the officers at their task here. I can assist them more than they realize. The Church can do more than the Fort to make these poor Mexicans 'good Americans.' And it is for the people's good; there is no other way in which they can better their condition.

"But this is not the day to write you of my duties or my purposes. To-night we are exiles, happy ones, thinking of home. Father Joseph has sent away our Mexican woman,—he will make a good cook of her in time, but to-night he is preparing our Christmas dinner himself. I had thought he would be worn out to-day, for he has been conducting a Novena of High Masses, as is the custom here before Christmas. After the Novena, and the midnight Mass last night, I supposed he would be willing to rest to-day; but not a bit of it. You know his motto, 'Rest in action.' I brought him a bottle of olive-oil on my horse all the way from Durango (I say 'olive-oil,' because here 'oil' means something to grease the wheels of wagons!), and he is making some sort of cooked salad. We have no green vegetables here in winter, and no one seems ever to have heard of that blessed plant, the lettuce. Joseph finds it hard to do without salad-oil, he always had it in Ohio, though it was a great extravagance. He has been in the kitchen all afternoon. There is only an open fire-place for cooking, and an earthen roasting-oven out in the court-yard. But he has never failed me in anything yet; and I think I can promise you that to-night two Frenchmen will sit down to a good dinner and drink your health."

The Bishop laid down his pen and lit his two candles with a splinter from the fire, then stood dusting his fingers by the deep-set window, looking out at the pale blue darkening sky. The evening-star hung above the amber afterglow, so soft, so brilliant that she seemed to bathe in her own silver light. *Ave Maris Stella,* the song which one of his friends at the Seminary used to intone so beautifully; humming it softly he returned to his desk and was just dipping his pen in the ink when the door opened, and a voice said,

"*Monseigneur est servi! Alors, Jean, veux-tu apporter les bougies?*"

The Bishop carried the candles into the dining-room, where the table was laid and Father Vaillant was changing his cook's apron for his cassock. Crimson from standing over an open fire, his rugged face was even homelier than usual—though one of the first things a stranger decided upon meeting Father Joseph was that the Lord had made few uglier men. He was short, skinny, bow-legged from a life on horseback, and his countenance had little to recommend it but kindliness and vivacity. He looked old, though he was then about forty. His skin was hardened and seamed by exposure to weather in a bitter climate, his neck scrawny and wrinkled like an old man's. A bold, blunt-tipped nose, positive chin, a very large mouth,—the lips thick and succulent but never loose, never relaxed, always stiffened by effort or working with excitement. His hair, sunburned to the shade of dry hay, had originally been tow-coloured; "*Blanchet*" ("Whitey") he was always called at the Seminary. Even his eyes were near-sighted, and of such a pale, watery blue as to be unimpressive. There was certainly nothing in his outer case to suggest the fierceness and fortitude and fire of the man, and yet even the thick-blooded Mexican half-breeds knew his quality at once. If the Bishop returned to find Santa Fé friendly to him, it was because everybody believed in Father Vaillant—homely, real, persistent, with the driving power of a dozen men in his poorly-built body.

On coming into the dining-room, Bishop Latour placed his candlesticks over the fire-place, since there were already six upon the table, illuminating the brown soup-pot. After they had stood for a moment in prayer, Father Joseph lifted the cover and ladled the soup into the plates, a dark onion soup with croutons. The Bishop tasted it critically and smiled at his companion. After the spoon had travelled to his lips a few times, he put it down and leaning back in his chair remarked,

"Think of it, *Blanchet;* in all this vast country between the Mississippi and the Pacific Ocean, there is probably not another human being who could make a soup like this."

"Not unless he is a Frenchman," said Father Joseph. He had tucked a napkin over the front of his cassock and was losing no time in reflection.

"I am not deprecating your individual talent, Joseph," the Bishop continued, "but, when one thinks of it, a soup like this is not the work of one man. It is the result of a constantly refined tradition. There are nearly a thousand years of history in this soup."

Father Joseph frowned intently at the earthen pot in the middle of the table. His pale, near-sighted eyes had always the look of peering into distance. "*C'est ça, c'est vrai,*" he murmured. "But how," he exclaimed as he filled the Bishop's plate again, "how can a man make a proper soup without leeks, that king of vegetables? We cannot go on eating onions for ever."

After carrying away the *soupière,* he brought in the roast chicken and *pommes sautées.* "And salad, Jean," he continued as he began to carve. "Are we to eat dried beans and roots for the rest of our lives? Surely we must find time to make a garden. Ah, my garden at Sandusky! And you could snatch me away from it! You will admit that you never ate better lettuces in France. And my vineyard; a natural habitat for the vine, that. I tell you, the shores of Lake Erie will be covered with vineyards one day. I envy the man who is drinking my wine. Ah well, that is a missionary's life; to plant where another shall reap."

As this was Christmas Day, the two friends were speaking in their native tongue. For years they had made it a practice to speak English together, except upon very special occasions, and of late they conversed in Spanish, in which they both needed to gain fluency.

"And yet sometimes you used to chafe a little at your dear Sandusky and its comforts," the Bishop reminded him—"to say that you would end a home-staying parish priest, after all."

"Of course, one wants to eat one's cake and have it, as they say in Ohio. But no farther, Jean. This is far enough. Do not drag me any farther." Father Joseph began gently to coax the cork from a bottle of red wine with his fingers. "This I begged for your dinner at the hacienda where I went to baptize the baby on St. Thomas's Day. It is not easy to separate these rich Mexicans from their French wine. They know its worth." He poured a few drops and tried it. "A slight taste of the cork; they do not know how to keep it properly. However, it is quite good enough for missionaries."

"You ask me not to drag you any farther, Joseph. I wish," Bishop Latour leaned back in his chair and locked his hands together beneath his chin, "I wish I knew how far this is! Does anyone know the extent of this diocese, or of this territory? The Commandant at the Fort seems as much in the dark as I. He says I can get some information from the scout, Kit Carson, who lives at Taos."

"Don't begin worrying about the diocese, Jean. For the present, Santa Fé is the diocese. Establish order at home. To-morrow I will have a reckoning with the church-wardens, who allowed that band of drunken cowboys to come in to the midnight Mass and defile the font. There is enough to do here. *Festina lente*. I have made a resolve not to go more than three days' journey from Santa Fé for one year."

The Bishop smiled and shook his head. "And when you were at the Seminary you made a resolve to lead a life of contemplation."

A light leaped into Father Joseph's homely face. "I have not yet renounced that hope. One day you will release me, and I will return to some religious house in France and end my days in devotion to the Holy Mother. For the time being, it is my destiny to serve Her in action. But this is far enough, Jean."

The Bishop again shook his head and murmured, "Who knows how far?"

The wiry little priest whose life was to be a succession of mountain ranges, pathless deserts, yawning canyons and swollen rivers, who was to carry the Cross into territories yet unknown and unnamed, who would wear down mules and horses and scouts and stage-drivers, tonight looked apprehensively at his superior and repeated, "No more, Jean. This is far enough." Then making haste to change the subject, he said briskly, "A bean salad was the best I could do for you; but with onion, and just a suspicion of salt pork, it is not so bad."

Over the compote of dried plums they fell to talking of the great yellow ones that grew in the old Latour garden at home. Their thoughts met in that tilted cobble street, winding down a hill, with the uneven garden walls and tall horse-chestnuts on either side; a lonely street after nightfall, with soft street lamps shaped like lanterns at the darkest turnings. At the end of it was the church where the Bishop made his first Communion, with a grove of flat-cut plane trees in front, under which the market was held on Tuesdays and Fridays.

While they lingered over these memories—an indulgence they seldom permitted themselves—the two missionaries were startled by a volley of rifle-shots and blood-curdling yells without, and the galloping of horses. The Bishop half rose, but Father Joseph reassured him with a shrug.

"Do not discompose yourself. The same thing happened here on the eve of All Souls' Day. A band of drunken cowboys, like those who came into the church last night, go out to the pueblo and get the Tesuque Indian boys drunk, and then they ride in to serenade the soldiers at the Fort in this manner."

4
A Bell and a Miracle

On the morning after the Bishop's return from Durango, after his first night in his Episcopal residence, he had a pleasant awakening from sleep. He had ridden into the court-yard after nightfall, having changed horses at a *rancho* and pushed on nearly sixty miles in order to reach home. Consequently he slept late the next morning—did not awaken until six o'clock, when he heard the Angelus ringing. He recovered consciousness slowly, unwilling to let go of a pleasing delusion that he was in Rome. Still half believing that he was lodged near St. John Lateran, he yet heard every stroke of the Ave Maria bell, marvelling to hear it rung correctly (nine quick strokes in all, divided into threes, with an interval between); and from a bell with beautiful tone. Full, clear, with something bland and suave, each note floated through the air like a globe of silver. Before the nine strokes were done Rome faded, and behind it he sensed something Eastern, with palm trees,—Jerusalem, perhaps, though he had never been there. Keeping his eyes closed, he cherished for a moment this sudden, pervasive sense of the East. Once before he had been carried out of the body thus to a place far away. It had happened in a street in New Orleans. He had turned a corner and come upon an old woman with a basket of yellow flowers; sprays of yellow sending out a honey-sweet perfume. Mimosa—but before he could think of the name he was overcome by a feeling of place, was dropped, cassock and all, into a garden in the south of France where he had been sent one winter in his childhood to recover from an illness. And now this silvery bell note had carried him farther and faster than sound could travel.

When he joined Father Vaillant at coffee, that impetuous man who could never keep a secret asked him anxiously whether he had heard anything.

"I thought I heard the Angelus, Father Joseph, but my reason tells me that only a long sea voyage could bring me within sound of such a bell."

"Not at all," said Father Joseph briskly. "I found that remarkable bell here, in the basement of old San Miguel. They tell me it has been here a hundred years or more. There is no church tower in the place strong enough to hold it—it is very thick and must weigh close upon eight hundred pounds. But I had a scaffolding built in the churchyard, and with the help of oxen we raised it and got it swung on cross-beams. I taught a Mexican boy to ring it properly against your return."

"But how could it have come here? It is Spanish, I suppose?"

"Yes, the inscription is in Spanish, to St. Joseph, and the date is 1356. It must have been brought up from Mexico City in an ox-cart. A heroic undertaking, certainly. Nobody knows where it was cast. But they do tell a story about it: that it was pledged to St. Joseph in the wars with the Moors, and that the people of some besieged city brought all their plate and silver and gold ornaments and threw them in with the baser metals. There is certainly a good deal of silver in the bell, nothing else would account for its tone."

Father Latour reflected. "And the silver of the Spaniards was really Moorish, was it not? If not actually of Moorish make, copied from their design. The Spaniards knew nothing about working silver except as they learned it from the Moors."

"What are you doing, Jean? Trying to make my bell out an infidel?" Father Joseph asked impatiently.

The Bishop smiled. "I am trying to account for the fact that when I heard it this morning it struck me at once as something oriental. A learned Scotch Jesuit in Montreal told me that our first bells, and the introduction of the bell in the service all over Europe, originally came from the East. He said the Templars brought the Angelus back from the Crusades, and it is really an adaptation of a Moslem custom."

Father Vaillant sniffed. "I noticed that scholars always manage to dig out something belittling," he complained.

"Belittling? I should say the reverse. I am glad to think there is Moorish silver in your bell. When we first came here, the one good workman we found in Santa Fé was a silversmith. The Spaniards handed on their skill to the Mexicans, and the Mexicans have taught the Navajos to work silver; but it all came from the Moors."

"I am no scholar, as you know," said Father Vaillant rising. "And this morning we have many practical affairs to occupy us. I have promised that you will give an audience to a good old man, a native priest from the Indian mission at Santa Clara, who is returning from Mexico. He has just been on a pilgrimage to the shrine of Our Lady of Guadalupe and has been much edified. He would like to tell you the story of his experience. It seems that ever since he was ordained he has desired to visit the shrine. During your absence I have found how particularly precious is that shrine to all Catholics in New Mexico. They regard it as the one absolutely authenticated appearance of the Blessed Virgin in the New World, and a witness of Her affection for Her Church on this continent."

The Bishop went into his study, and Father Vaillant brought in Padre Escolastico Herrera, a man of nearly seventy, who had been forty years in the ministry, and had just accomplished the pious desire of a lifetime. His mind was still full of the sweetness of his late experience. He was so rapt that nothing else interested him. He asked anxiously whether perhaps the Bishop would have more leisure to attend to him later in the day. But Father Latour placed a chair for him and told him to proceed.

The old man thanked him for the privilege of being seated. Leaning forward, with his hands locked between his knees, he told the whole story of the miraculous appearance, both because it was so dear to his heart, and because he was sure that no "American" Bishop would have heard of the occurrence as it was, though at Rome all the details were well known and two Popes had sent gifts to the shrine.

On Saturday, December 9th, in the year 1531, a poor neophyte of the monastery of St. James was hurrying down Tapeyac hill to attend Mass in the City of Mexico. His name was Juan Diego and he was fifty-five years old. When he was half way down the hill a light shone in his path, and the Mother of God appeared to him as a young woman of great beauty, clad in blue and gold. She greeted him by name and said:

"Juan, seek out thy Bishop and bid him build a church in my honour on the spot where I now stand. Go then, and I will bide here and await thy return."

Brother Juan ran into the City and straight to the Bishop's palace, where he reported the matter. The Bishop was Zumarraga, a Spaniard. He questioned the monk severely and told him he should have required a sign of the Lady to assure him that she was indeed the Mother of God and not some evil spirit. He dismissed the poor brother harshly and set an attendant to watch his actions.

Juan went forth very downcast and repaired to the house of his uncle, Bernardino, who was sick of a fever. The two succeeding days he spent in caring for this aged man who seemed at the point of death. Because of the Bishop's reproof he had fallen into doubt, and did not return to the spot where the Lady said She would await him. On Tuesday he left the City to go back to his monastery to fetch medicines for Bernardino, but he avoided the place where he had seen the vision and went by another way.

Again he saw a light in his path and the Virgin appeared to him as before, saying, "Juan, why goest thou by this way?"

Weeping, he told Her that the Bishop had distrusted his report, and that he had been employed in caring for his uncle, who was sick unto death. The Lady spoke to him with all comfort, telling him that his uncle would be healed within the hour, and that he should return to Bishop Zumarraga and bid him build a church where She had first appeared to him. It must be called the shrine of Our Lady of Guadalupe, after Her dear shrine of that name in Spain. When Brother Juan replied to Her that the Bishop required a sign, She said: "Go up on the rocks yonder, and gather roses."

Though it was December and not the season for roses, he ran up among the rocks and found such roses as he had never seen before. He gathered them until he had filled his *tilma*. The *tilma* was a mantle worn only by the very poor,—a wretched garment loosely woven of coarse vegetable fibre and sewn down the middle. When he returned to the apparition, She bent over the flowers and took pains to arrange them, then closed the ends of the *tilma* together and said to him:

"Go now, and do not open your mantle until you open it before your Bishop."

Juan sped into the City and gained admission to the Bishop, who was in council with his Vicar.

"Your Grace," he said, "the Blessed Lady who appeared to me has sent you these roses for a sign."

At this he held up one end of his *tilma* and let the roses fall in profusion to the floor. To his astonishment, Bishop Zumarraga and his Vicar instantly fell upon their knees among the flowers. On the inside of his poor mantle was a painting of the Blessed Virgin, in robes of blue and rose and gold, exactly as She had appeared to him upon the hillside.

A shrine was built to contain this miraculous portrait, which since that day has been the goal of countless pilgrimages and has performed many miracles.

Of this picture Padre Escolastico had much to say: he affirmed that it was of marvellous beauty, rich with gold, and the colours as pure and delicate as the tints of early morning. Many painters had visited the shrine and marvelled that paint could be laid at all upon such poor and coarse material. In the ordinary way of nature, the flimsy mantle would have fallen to pieces long ago. The Padre modestly presented Bishop Latour and Father Joseph with little medals he had brought from the shrine; on one side a relief of the miraculous portrait, on the other an inscription: *Non fecit taliter omni nationi*. (*She hath not dealt so with any nation.*)

Father Vaillant was deeply stirred by the priest's recital, and after the old man had gone he declared to the Bishop that he meant himself to make a pilgrimage to this shrine at the earliest opportunity.

"What a priceless thing for the poor converts of a savage country!" he exclaimed, wiping his glasses, which were clouded by his strong feeling. "All these poor Catholics who have been so long without instruction have at least the reassurance of that visitation. It is a household word with them that their Blessed Mother revealed Herself in their own country, to a poor convert. Doctrine is well enough for the wise, Jean; but the miracle is something we can hold in our hands and love."

Father Vaillant began pacing restlessly up and down as he spoke, and the Bishop watched him, musing. It was just this in his friend that was dear to him. "Where there is great love there are always miracles," he said at length. "One might almost say that an apparition is human vision corrected by divine love. I do not see you as you really are, Joseph; I see you through my affection for you. The Miracles of the Church seem to me to rest not so much upon faces or voices or healing power coming suddenly near to us from afar off, but upon our perceptions being made finer, so that for a moment our eyes can see and our ears can hear what is there about us always."

BOOK TWO

Missionary Journeys

1
The White Mules

In mid-March, Father Vaillant was on the road, returning from a missionary journey to Albuquerque. He was to stop at the *rancho* of a rich Mexican, Manuel Lujon, to marry his men and maid servants who were living in concubinage, and to baptize the children. There he would spend the night. To-morrow or the day after he would go on to Santa Fé, halting by the way at the Indian pueblo of Santo Domingo to hold service. There was a fine old mission church at Santo Domingo, but the Indians were of a haughty and suspicious disposition. He had said Mass there on his way to Albuquerque, nearly a week ago. By dint of canvassing from house to house, and offering medals and religious colour prints to all who came to church, he had got together a considerable congregation. It was a large and prosperous pueblo, set among clean sand-hills, with its rich irrigated farm lands lying just below, in the valley of the Rio Grande. His congregation was quiet, dignified, attentive. They sat on the earth floor, wrapped in their best blankets, repose in every line of their strong, stubborn backs. He harangued them in such Spanish as he could command, and they listened with respect. But bring their children to be baptized, they would not. The Spaniards had treated them very badly long ago, and they had been meditating upon their grievance for many generations. Father Vaillant had not baptized one infant there, but he meant to stop to-morrow and try again. Then back to his Bishop, provided he could get his horse up La Bajada Hill.

He had bought his horse from a Yankee trader and had been woefully deceived. One week's journey of from twenty to thirty miles a day had shown the beast up for a wind-broken wreck. Father Vaillant's mind was full of material cares as he approached Manuel Lujon's place beyond Bernalillo. The *rancho* was like a little town, with all its stables, corrals, and stake fences. The *casa grande* was long and low, with glass windows and bright blue doors a *portale* running its full length, supported by blue posts. Under this *portale* the adobe wall was hung with bridles, saddles, great boots and spurs, guns and saddle blankets, strings of red peppers, fox skins, and the skins of two great rattlesnakes.

When Father Vaillant rode in through the gateway, children came running from every direction, some with no clothing but a little shirt, and women with no shawls over their black hair came running after the children. They all disappeared when Manuel Lujon walked out of the great house,

MISSIONARY JOURNEYS **31**

hat in hand, smiling and hospitable. He was a man of thirty-five, settled in figure and somewhat full under the chin. He greeted the priest in the name of God and put out a hand to help him alight, but Father Vaillant sprang quickly to the ground.

"God be with you, Manuel, and with your house. But where are those who are to be married?"

"The men are all in the field, Padre. There is no hurry. A little wine, a little bread, coffee, repose—and then the ceremonies."

"A little wine, very willingly, and bread, too. But not until afterward. I meant to catch you all at dinner, but I am two hours late because my horse is bad. Have someone bring in my saddle-bags, and I will put on my vestments. Send out to the fields for your men, Señor Lujon. A man can stop work to be married."

The swarthy host was dazed by this dispatch. "But one moment, Padre. There are all the children to baptize; why not begin with them, if I cannot persuade you to wash the dust from your sainted brow and repose a little."

"Take me to a place where I can wash and change my clothes, and I will be ready before you can get them here. No, I tell you, Lujon, the marriages first, the baptisms afterward; that order is but Christian. I will baptize the children to-morrow morning, and their parents will at least have been married over night."

Father Joseph was conducted to his chamber, and the older boys were sent running off across the fields to fetch the men. Lujon and his two daughters began constructing an altar at one end of the *sala*. Two old women came to scrub the floor, and another brought chairs and stools.

"My God, but he is ugly, the Padre!" whispered one of these to the other. "He must be very holy. And did you see the great wart he has on his chin? My grandmother could take that away for him if she were alive, poor soul! Somebody ought to tell him about the holy mud at Chimayo. That mud might dry it up. But there is nobody left now who can take warts away."

"No, the times are not so good any more," the other agreed. "And I doubt if all this marrying will make them any better. Of what use is it to marry people after they have lived together and had children? and the man is maybe thinking about another woman, like Pablo. I saw him coming out of the brush with that oldest girl of Trinidad's, only Sunday night."

The reappearance of the priest upon the scene cut short further scandal. He knelt down before the improvised altar and began his private devotions. The women tiptoed away. Señor Lujon himself went out toward the servants' quarters to hurry the candidates for the marriage sacrament. The women were giggling and snatching up their best shawls. Some of the men had even washed their hands. The household crowded into the *sala*, and Father Vaillant married couples with great dispatch.

"To-morrow morning, the baptisms," he announced. "And the mothers see to it that the children are clean, and that there are sponsors for all."

After he had resumed his travelling-clothes, Father Joseph asked his host at what hour he dined, remarking that he had been fasting since an early breakfast.

"We eat when it is ready—a little after sunset, usually. I have had a young lamb killed for your Reverence."

Father Joseph kindled with interest. "Ah, and how will it be cooked?"

Señor Lujon shrugged. "Cooked? Why, they put it in a pot with chili, and some onions, I suppose."

"Ah, that is the point. I have had too much stewed mutton. Will you permit me to go into the kitchen and cook my portion in my own way?"

Lujon waved his hand. "My house is yours, Padre. Into the kitchen I never go—too many women. But there it is, and the woman in charge is Rosa."

When the Father entered the kitchen he found a crowd of women discussing the marriages. They quickly dispersed, leaving old Rosa by her fire-place, where hung a kettle from which issued the savour of cooking mutton fat, all too familiar to Father Joseph. He found a half sheep hanging outside the door, covered with a bloody sack, and asked Rosa to heat the oven for him, announcing that he meant to roast the hind leg.

"But Padre, I baked before the marriages. The oven is almost cold. It will take an hour to heat it, and it is only two hours till supper."

"Very well, I can cook my roast in an hour."

"Cook a roast in an hour!" cried the old woman. "Mother of God, Padre, the blood will not be dried in it!"

"Not if I can help it!" said Father Joseph fiercely. "Now hurry with the fire, my good woman."

When the Padre carved his roast at the supper-table, the serving-girls stood behind his chair and looked with horror at the delicate stream of pink juice that followed the knife. Manuel Lujon took a slice for politeness, but he did not eat it. Father Vaillant had his *gigot* to himself.

All the men and boys sat down at the long table with the host, the women and children would eat later. Father Joseph and Lujon, at one end, had a bottle of white Bordeaux between them. It had been brought from Mexico City on mule-back, Lujon said. They were discussing the road back to Santa Fé, and when the missionary remarked that he would stop at Santo Domingo, the host asked him why he did not get a horse there. "I am afraid you will hardly get back to Santa Fé on your own. The pueblo is famous for breeding good horses. You might make a trade."

"No," said Father Vaillant. "Those Indians are of a sullen disposition. If I were to have dealings with them, they would suspect my motives. If we are to save their souls, we must make it clear that we want no profit for ourselves, as I told Father Gallegos in Albuquerque."

Manuel Lujon laughed and glanced down the table at his men, who were all showing their white teeth. "You said that to the Padre at Albuquerque? You have courage. He is a rich man, Padre Gallegos. All the same, I respect him. I have played poker with him. He is a great gambler and takes his losses like a man. He stops at nothing, plays like an American."

"And I," retorted Father Joseph, "I have not much respect for a priest who either plays cards or manages to get rich."

"Then you do not play?" asked Lujon. "I am disappointed. I had hoped we could have a game after supper. The evenings are dull enough here. You do not even play dominoes?"

"Ah, that is another matter!" Father Joseph declared. "A game of dominoes, there by the fire, with coffee, or some of that excellent grape brandy you allowed me to taste, that I would find refreshing. And tell me, Manuelito, where do you get that brandy? It is like a French liqueur."

"It is well seasoned. It was made at Bernalillo in my grandfather's time. They make it there still, but it is not so good now."

The next morning, after coffee, while the children were being got ready for baptism, the host took Father Vaillant through his corrals and stables to show him his stock. He exhibited with peculiar pride two cream-coloured mules, stalled side by side. With his own hand he led them out of the stable, in order to display to advantage their handsome coats,—not bluish white, as with white horses, but a rich, deep ivory, that in shadow changed to fawn-colour. Their tails were clipped at the end into the shape of bells.

"Their names," said Lujon, "are Contento and Angelica, and they are as good as their names. It seems that God has given them intelligence. When I talk to them, they look up at me like Christians; they are very companionable. They are always ridden together and have a great affection for each other."

Father Joseph took one by the halter and led it about. "Ah, but they are rare creatures! I have never seen a mule or horse coloured like a young fawn before." To his host's astonishment, the wiry little priest sprang upon Contento's back with the agility of a grasshopper. The mule, too, was astonished. He shook himself violently, bolted toward the gate of the barnyard, and at the gate stopped suddenly. Since this did not throw his rider, he seemed satisfied, trotted back, and stood placidly beside Angelica.

"But you are a *cabalerro*, Father Vaillant!" Lujon exclaimed. "I doubt if Father Gallegos would have kept his seat—though he is something of a hunter."

"The saddle is to be my home in your country, Lujon. What an easy gait this mule has, and what a narrow back! I notice that especially. For a man with short legs, like me, it is a punishment to ride eight hours a day on a wide horse. And this I must do day after day. From here I go to Santa Fé, and after a day in conference with the Bishop, I start for Mora."

"For Mora?" exclaimed Lujon. "Yes, that is far, and the roads are very bad. On your mare you will never do it. She will drop dead under you." While he talked the Father remained upon the mule's back, stroking him with his hand.

"Well, I have no other. God grant that she does not drop somewhere far from food and water. I can carry very little with me except my vestments and the sacred vessels."

The Mexican had been growing more and more thoughtful, as if he were considering something profound and not altogether cheerful. Suddenly his brow cleared, and he turned to the priest with a radiant smile, quite boyish in its simplicity. "Father Vaillant," he burst out in a slightly oratorical manner, "you have made my house right with Heaven, and you charge me very little. I will do something very nice for you; I will give you Contento for a present, and I hope to be particularly remembered in your prayers."

Springing to the ground, Father Vaillant threw his arms about his host. "Manuelito!" he cried, "for this darling mule I think I could almost pray you into Heaven!"

The Mexican laughed, too, and warmly returned the embrace. Arm-in-arm they went in to begin the baptisms.

The next morning, when Lujon went to call Father Vaillant for breakfast, he found him in the barnyard, leading the two mules about and smoothing their fawn-coloured flanks, but his face was not the cheerful countenance of yesterday.

"Manuel," he said at once, "I cannot accept your present. I have thought upon it over night, and I see that I cannot. The Bishop works as hard as I do, and his horse is little better than mine. You know he lost everything on his way out here, in a shipwreck at Galveston—among the rest a fine wagon he had had built for travel on these plains. I could not go about on a mule like this when my Bishop rides a common hack. It would be inappropriate. I must ride away on my old mare."

"Yes, Padre?" Manuel looked troubled and somewhat aggrieved. Why should the Padre spoil everything? It had all been very pleasant yesterday, and he had felt like a prince of generosity. "I doubt if she will make La Bajada Hill," he said slowly, shaking his head. "Look my horses over and take the one that suits you. They are all better than yours."

"No, no," said Father Vaillant decidedly. "Having seen these mules, I want nothing else. They are the colour of pearls, really! I will raise the price of marriages until I can buy this pair from you. A missionary must depend upon his mount for companionship in his lonely life. I want a mule that can look at me like a Christian, as you said of these."

Señor Lujon sighed and looked about his barnyard as if he were trying to find some escape from this situation.

Father Joseph turned to him with vehemence. "If I were a rich *ranchero*, like you, Manuel, I would do a splendid thing; I would furnish the two mounts that are to carry the word of God about this heathen country, and then I would say to myself: *There go my Bishop and my Vicario, on my beautiful cream-coloured mules.*"

"So be it, Padre," said Lujon with a mournful smile. "But I ought to get a good many prayers. On my whole estate there is nothing I prize like those two. True, they might pine if they were parted for long. They have never been separated, and they have a great affection for each other. Mules, as you know, have strong affections. It is hard for me to give them up."

"You will be all the happier for that, Manuelito," Father Joseph cried heartily. "Every time you think of these mules, you will feel pride in your good deed."

Soon after breakfast Father Vaillant departed, riding Contento, with Angelica trotting submissively behind, and from his gate Señor Lujon watched them disconsolately until they disappeared. He felt he had been worried out of his mules, and yet he bore no resentment. He did not doubt Father Joseph's devotedness, nor his singleness of purpose. After all, a Bishop was a Bishop, and a Vicar was a Vicar, and it was not to their discredit that they worked like a pair of common parish priests. He believed he would be proud of the fact that they rode Contento and Angelica. Father Vaillant had forced his hand, but he was rather glad of it.

2
The Lonely Road to Mora

The Bishop and his Vicar were riding through the rain in the Truchas mountains. The heavy, lead-coloured drops were driven slantingly through the air by an icy wind from the peak. These raindrops, Father Latour kept thinking, were the shape of tadpoles, and they broke against his nose and cheeks, exploding with a splash, as if they were hollow and full of air. The priests were riding across high mountain meadows, which in a few weeks would be green, though just now they were slate-coloured. On every side lay ridges covered with blue-green fir trees; above them rose the horny backbones of mountains. The sky was very low; purplish lead-coloured clouds let down curtains of mist into the valleys between the pine ridges. There was not a glimmer of white light in the dark vapours working overhead—rather, they took on the cold green of the evergreens. Even the white mules, their coats wet and matted into tufts, had turned a slaty hue, and the faces of the two priests were purple and spotted in that singular light.

Father Latour rode first, sitting straight upon his mule, with his chin lowered just enough to keep the drive of rain out of his eyes. Father Vaillant followed, unable to see much,—in weather like this his glasses were of no use, and he had taken them off. He crouched down in the saddle, his shoulders well over Contento's neck. Father Joseph's sister, Philomène, who was Mother Superior of a convent in her native town in the Puy-de-Dôme, often tried to picture her brother and Bishop Latour on these long missionary journeys of which he wrote her; she imagined the scene and saw the two priests moving through it in their cassocks, bareheaded, like the pictures of St. Francis Xavier with which she was familiar. The reality was less picturesque,—but for all that, no one could have mistaken these two men for hunters or traders. They wore clerical collars about their necks instead of neckerchiefs, and on the breast of his buckskin jacket the Bishop's silver cross hung by a silver chain.

They were on their way to Mora, the third day out, and they did not know just how far they had still to go. Since morning they had not met a traveller or seen a human habitation. They believed they were on the right trail, for they had seen no other. The first night of their journey they had spent at Santa Cruz, lying in the warm, wide valley of the Rio Grande, where the fields and gardens were already softly coloured with early spring. But since they had left the Española country behind them, they had contended first with wind and sand-storms, and now with cold. The Bishop was going to Mora to assist the Padre there in disposing of a crowd of refugees who filled his house. A new settlement in the Conejos valley had lately been raided by Indians; many of the inhabitants were killed, and the survivors, who were originally from Mora, had managed to get back there, utterly destitute.

Before the travellers had crossed the mountain meadows, the rain turned to sleet. Their wet buckskins quickly froze, and the rattle of icy flakes struck them and bounded off. The prospect of a night in the open was not cheering. It was too wet to kindle a fire, their blankets would become soaked on the ground. As they were descending the mountain on the Mora side, the grey daylight seemed already beginning to fail, though it was only four o'clock. Father Latour turned in his saddle and spoke over his shoulder.

"The mules are certainly very tired, Joseph. They ought to be fed."

"Push on," said Father Vaillant. "We will come to shelter of some kind before night sets in." The Vicar had been praying steadfastly while they crossed the meadows, and he felt confident that St. Joseph would not turn a deaf ear. Before the hour was done they did indeed come upon a wretched adobe house, so poor and mean that they might not have seen it had it not lain close beside the trail, on the edge of a steep ravine. The stable looked more habitable than the house, and the priests thought perhaps they could spend the night in it.

As they rode up to the door, a man came out, bareheaded, and they saw to their surprise that he was not a Mexican, but an American, of a very unprepossessing type. He spoke to them in some drawling dialect they could scarcely understand and asked if they wanted to stay the night. During the few words they exchanged with him Father Latour felt a growing reluctance to remain even for a few hours under the roof of this ugly, evil-looking fellow. He was tall, gaunt and ill-formed, with a snake-like neck, terminating in a small, bony head. Under his close-clipped hair this repellent head showed a number of thick ridges, as if the skull joinings were overgrown by layers of superfluous bone. With its small, rudimentary ears, this head had a positively malignant look. The man seemed not more than half human, but he was the only householder on the lonely road to Mora.

The priests dismounted and asked him whether he could put their mules under shelter and give them grain feed.

"As soon as I git my coat on I will. You kin come in."

They followed him into a room where a piñon fire blazed in the corner, and went toward it to warm their stiffened hands. Their host made an angry, snarling sound in the direction of the partition, and a woman came out of the next room. She was a Mexican.

Father Latour and Father Vaillant addressed her courteously in Spanish, greeting her in the name of the holy Mother, as was customary. She did not open her lips, but stared at them blankly for a moment, then dropped her eyes and cowered as if she were terribly frightened. The priests looked at each other; it struck them both that this man had been abusing her in some way. Suddenly he turned on her.

"Clear off them cheers fur the strangers. They won't eat ye, if they air priests."

She began distractedly snatching rags and wet socks and dirty clothes from the chairs. Her hands were shaking so that she dropped things. She was not old, she might have been very young, but she was probably half-witted. There was nothing in her face but blankness and fear.

Her husband put on his coat and boots, went to the door, and stopped with his hand on the latch, throwing over his shoulder a crafty, hateful glance at the bewildered woman.

"Here, you! Come right along, I'll need ye!"

She took her black shawl from a peg and followed him. Just at the door she turned and caught the eyes of the visitors, who were looking after her in compassion and perplexity. Instantly that stupid face became intense, prophetic, full of awful meaning. With her finger she pointed them away,

away!—two quick thrusts into the air. Then, with a look of horror beyond anything language could convey, she threw back her head and drew the edge of her palm quickly across her distended throat—and vanished. The doorway was empty; the two priests stood staring at it, speechless. That flash of electric passion had been so swift, the warning it communicated so vivid and definite, that they were struck dumb.

Father Joseph was the first to find his tongue. "There is no doubt of her meaning. Your pistol is loaded, Jean?"

"Yes, but I neglected to keep it dry. No matter."

They hurried out of the house. It was still light enough to see the stable through the grey drive of rain, and they went toward it.

"Señor American," the Bishop called, "will you be good enough to bring out our mules?"

The man came out of the stable. "What do you want?"

"Our mules. We have changed our mind. We will push on to Mora. And here is a dollar for your trouble."

The man took a threatening attitude. As he looked from one to the other his head played from side to side exactly like a snake's. "What's the matter? My house ain't good enough for ye?"

"No explanation is necessary. Go into the barn and get the mules, Father Joseph."

"You dare go into my stable, you——priest!"

The Bishop drew his pistol. "No profanity, Señor. We want nothing from you but to get away from your uncivil tongue. Stand where you are."

The man was unarmed. Father Joseph came out with the mules, which had not been unsaddled. The poor things were each munching a mouthful, but they needed no urging to be gone; they did not like this place. The moment they felt their riders on their backs they trotted quickly along the road, which dropped immediately into the arroyo. While they were descending, Father Joseph remarked that the man would certainly have a gun in the house, and that he had no wish to be shot in the back.

"Nor I. But it is growing too dark for that, unless he should follow us on horseback," said the Bishop. "Were there horses in the stable?"

"Only a burro." Father Vaillant was relying upon the protection of St. Joseph, whose office he had fervently said that morning. The warning given them by that poor woman, with such scant opportunity, seemed evidence that some protecting power was mindful of them.

By the time they had ascended the far side of the arroyo, night had closed down and the rain was pouring harder than ever.

"I am by no means sure that we can keep in the road," said the Bishop. "But at least I am sure we are not being followed. We must trust to these intelligent beasts. Poor woman! He will suspect her and abuse her,

I am afraid." He kept seeing her in the darkness as he rode on, her face in the fire-light, and her terrible pantomime.

They reached the town of Mora a little after midnight. The Padre's house was full of refugees, and two of them were put out of a bed in order that the Bishop and his Vicar could get into it.

In the morning a boy came from the stable and reported that he had found a crazy woman lying in the straw, and that she begged to see the two Padres who owned the white mules. She was brought in, her clothing cut to rags, her legs and face and even her hair so plastered with mud that the priests could scarcely recognize the woman who had saved their lives the night before.

She said she had never gone back to the house at all. When the two priests rode away her husband had run to the house to get his gun, and she had plunged down a washout behind the stable into the arroyo, and had been on the way to Mora all night. She had supposed he would overtake her and kill her, but he had not. She reached the settlement before day-break, and crept into the stable to warm herself among the animals and wait until the household was awake. Kneeling before the Bishop she began to relate such horrible things that he stopped her and turned to the native priest.

"This is a case for the civil authorities. Is there a magistrate here?"

There was no magistrate, but there was a retired fur trapper who acted as notary and could take evidence. He was sent for, and in the interval Father Latour instructed the refugee women from Conejos to bathe this poor creature and put decent clothes on her, and to care for the cuts and scratches on her legs.

An hour later the woman, whose name was Magdalena, calmed by food and kindness, was ready to tell her story. The notary had brought along his friend, St. Vrain, a Canadian trapper who understood Spanish better than he. The woman was known to St. Vrain, moreover, who confirmed her statement that she was born Magdalena Valdez, at Los Ranchos de Taos, and that she was twenty-four years old. Her husband, Buck Scales, had drifted into Taos with a party of hunters from somewhere in Wyoming. All white men knew him for a dog and a degenerate—but to Mexican girls, marriage with an American meant coming up in the world. She had married him six years ago, and had been living with him ever since in that wretched house on the Mora trail. During that time he had robbed and murdered four travellers who had stopped there for the night. They were all strangers, not known in the country. She had forgot their names, but one was a German boy who spoke very little Spanish and little English; a nice boy with blue eyes, and she had grieved for him more than for the others. They were all buried in the sandy soil behind the stable. She was always afraid their bodies might wash out in a storm. Their horses Buck had ridden off by night and sold to Indians somewhere in the north. Magdalena had borne three children since her marriage, and her husband had killed each of them a few days after birth, by ways so horrible that she could not relate it. After he killed the first baby, she ran away from him, back to her parents at Ranchos. He came after her and made her go home with him by threatening harm to the old people. She was afraid to go anywhere for help, but twice before she had managed to warn travellers away, when her husband happened to be out of the house. This time she had found courage because, when she looked into the faces of these two Padres, she knew they were good men, and she thought if she ran after them they could save her. She could not bear any more killing. She asked nothing better than to die herself, if only she could hide near a church and a priest for a while, to make her soul right with God.

St. Vrain and his friend got together a search-party at once. They rode out to Scales's place and found the remains of four men buried under the corral behind the stable, as the woman had said. Scales himself they captured on the road from Taos, where he had gone to look for his wife. They brought him back to Mora, but St. Vrain rode on to Taos to fetch a magistrate.

There was no *calabozo* in Mora, so Scales was put into an empty stable, under guard. This stable was soon surrounded by a crowd of people, who loitered to hear the blood-curdling threats the prisoner shouted against his wife. Magdalena was kept in the Padre's house, where she lay on a mat in the corner, begging Father Latour to take her back to Santa Fé, so that her husband could not get at her. Though Scales was bound, the Bishop felt alarmed for her safety. He and the American notary, who had a pistol of the new revolver model, sat in the *sala* and kept watch over her all night.

In the morning the magistrate and his party arrived from Taos. The notary told him the facts of the case in the plaza, where everyone could hear. The Bishop inquired whether there was any place for Magdalena in Taos, as she could not stay on here in such a state of terror.

A man dressed in buckskin hunting-clothes stepped out of the crowd and asked to see Magdalena. Father Latour conducted him into the room where she lay on her mat. The stranger went up to her, removing his hat. He bent down and put his hand on her shoulder. Though he was clearly an American, he spoke Spanish in the native manner.

"Magdalena, don't you remember me?"

She looked up at him as out of a dark well; something became alive in her deep, haunted eyes. She caught with both hands at his fringed buckskin knees.

"Christóbal!" she wailed. "Oh, Christóbal!"

"I'll take you home with me, Magdalena, and you can stay with my wife. You wouldn't be afraid in my house, would you?"

"No, no, Christóbal, I would not be afraid with you. I am not a wicked woman."

He smoothed her hair. "You're a good girl, Magdalena—always were. It will be all right. Just leave things to me."

Then he turned to the Bishop. "Señor Vicario, she can come to me. I live near Taos. My wife is a native woman, and she'll be good to her. That varmint won't come about my place, even if he breaks jail. He knows me. My name is Carson."

Father Latour had looked forward to meeting the scout. He had supposed him to be a very large man, of powerful body and commanding presence. This Carson was not so tall as the Bishop himself, was very slight in frame, modest in manner, and he spoke English with a soft Southern drawl. His face was both thoughtful and alert; anxiety had drawn a permanent ridge between his blue eyes. Under his blond moustache his mouth had a singular refinement. The lips were full and delicately modelled. There was something curiously unconscious about his mouth, reflective, a little melancholy,—and something that suggested a capacity for tenderness. The Bishop felt a quick glow of pleasure in looking at the man. As he stood there in his buckskin clothes one felt in him standards, loyalties, a code which is not easily put into words but which is instantly felt when two men who live by it come together by chance. He took the scout's hand. "I have long wanted to meet Kit Carson," he said, "even before I came to New Mexico. I have been hoping you would pay me a visit at Santa Fé."

The other smiled. "I'm right shy, sir, and I'm always afraid of being disappointed. But I guess it will be all right from now on."

This was the beginning of a long friendship.

On their ride back to Carson's ranch, Magdalena was put in Father Vaillant's care, and the Bishop and the scout rode together. Carson said he had become a Catholic merely as a matter of form, as Americans usually did when they married a Mexican girl. His wife was a good woman and very devout; but religion had seemed to him pretty much a woman's affair until his last trip to California. He had been sick out there, and the Fathers at one of the missions took care of him. "I began to see things different, and thought I might some day be a Catholic in earnest. I was brought up to think priests were rascals, and that the nuns were bad women,—all the stuff they talk back in Missouri. A good many of the native priests here bear out that story. Our Padre Martínez at Taos is an old scapegrace, if ever there was one; he's got children and grandchildren in almost every settlement around here. And Padre Lucero at Arroyo Hondo is a miser, takes everything a poor man's got to give him a Christian burial."

The Bishop discussed the needs of his people at length with Carson. He felt great confidence in his judgment. The two men were about the same age, both a little over forty, and both had been sobered and sharpened by wide experience. Carson had been a guide in world-renowned explorations, but he was still almost as poor as in the days when he was a beaver trapper. He lived in a little adobe house with his Mexican wife. The great country of desert and mountain ranges between Santa Fé and the Pacific coast was not yet mapped or charted; the most reliable map of it was in Kit Carson's brain. This Missourian, whose eye was so quick to read a landscape or a human face, could not read a printed page. He could at that time barely write his own name. Yet one felt in him a quick and discriminating intelligence. That he was illiterate was an accident; he had got ahead of books, gone where the printing-press could not follow him. Out of the hardships of his boyhood—from fourteen to twenty picking up a bare living as cook or mule-driver for wagon trains, often in the service of brutal and desperate characters—he had preserved a clean sense of honour and a compassionate heart. In talking to the Bishop of poor Magdalena he said sadly: "I used to see her in Taos when she was such a pretty girl. Ain't it a pity?"

The degenerate murderer, Buck Scales, was hanged after a short trial. Early in April the Bishop left Santa Fé on horseback and rode to St. Louis, on his way to attend the Provincial Council at Baltimore. When he returned in September, he brought back with him five courageous nuns, Sisters of Loretto, to found a school for girls in letterless Santa Fé. He sent at once for Magdalena and took her into the service of the Sisters. She became housekeeper and manager of the Sisters' kitchen. She was devoted to the nuns, and so happy in the service of the Church that when the Bishop visited the school he used to enter by the kitchen-garden in order to see her serene and handsome face. For she became beautiful, as Carson said she had been as a girl. After the blight of her horrible youth was over, she seemed to bloom again in the household of God.

Death Comes for the Archbishop

Book Three

The Mass at Ácoma

1
The Wooden Parrot

During the first year after his arrival in Santa Fé, the Bishop was actually in his diocese only about four months. Six months of that first year were consumed in attending the Plenary Council at Baltimore, to which he had been summoned. He went on horseback over the Santa Fé trail to St. Louis, nearly a thousand miles, then by steamboat to Pittsburgh, across the mountains to Cumberland, and on to Washington by the new railroad. The return journey was even slower, as he had with him the five nuns who came to found the school of Our Lady of Light. He reached Santa Fé late in September.

So far, Bishop Latour had been mainly employed on business that took him far away from his Vicarate. His great diocese was still an unimaginable mystery to him. He was eager to be abroad in it, to know his people; to escape for a little from the cares of building and founding, and to go westward among the old isolated Indian missions; Santo Domingo, breeder of horses; Isleta, whitened with gypsum; Laguna, of wide pastures; and finally, cloud-set Ácoma.

In the golden October weather the Bishop, with his blankets and coffee-pot, attended by Jacinto, a young Indian from the Pecos pueblo, whom he employed as guide, set off to visit the Indian missions in the west. He spent a night and a day at Albuquerque, with the genial and popular Padre Gallegos. After Santa Fé, Albuquerque was the most important parish in the diocese; the priest belonged to an influential Mexican family, and he and the *rancheros* had run their church to suit themselves, making a very gay affair of it. Though Padre Gallegos was ten years older than the Bishop, he would still dance the fandango five nights running, as if he could never have enough of it. He had many friends in the American colony, with whom he played poker and went hunting, when he was not dancing with the Mexicans. His cellar was well stocked with wines from El Paso del Norte, whiskey from Taos, and grape brandy from Bernalillo. He was genuinely hospitable, and the gambler down on his luck, the soldier sobering up, were always welcome at his table. The Padre was adored by a rich Mexican widow, who was hostess at his supper parties, engaged his servants for him, made lace for the altar and napery for his table. Every Sunday her carriage, the only closed one in Albuquerque, waited in the plaza after Mass, and when the priest had put off his vestments, he came out and was driven away to the lady's hacienda for dinner.

The Bishop and Father Vaillant had thoroughly examined the case of Father Gallegos, and meant to end this scandalous state of things well before Christmas. But on this visit Father Latour exhibited neither astonishment nor displeasure at anything, and Padre Gallegos was cordial and most ceremoniously polite. When the Bishop permitted himself to express some surprise that there was not a confirmation class awaiting him, the Padre explained smoothly that it was his custom to confirm infants at their baptism.

"It is all the same in a Christian community like ours. We know they will receive religious instruction as they grow up, so we make good Catholics of them in the beginning. Why not?"

The Padre was uneasy lest the Bishop should require his attendance on this trip out among the missions. He had no liking for scanty food and a bed on the rocks. So, though he had been dancing only a few nights before, he received his Superior with one foot bandaged up in an Indian moccasin, and complained of a severe attack of gout. Asked when he had last celebrated Mass at Ácoma, he made no direct reply. It used to be his custom, he said, to go there in Passion Week, but the Ácoma Indians were unreclaimed heathen at heart, and had no wish to be bothered with the Mass. The last time he went out there, he was unable to get into the church at all. The Indians pretended they had not the key; that the Governor had it, and that he had gone on "Indian business" up into the Cebolleta mountains.

The Bishop did not wish Padre Gallegos's company upon his journey, was very glad not to have the embarrassment of refusing it, and he rode away from Albuquerque after polite farewells. Yet, he reflected, there was something very engaging about Gallegos as a man. As a priest, he was impossible; he was too self-satisfied and popular ever to change his ways, and he certainly could not change his face. He did not look quite like a professional gambler, but something smooth and twinkling in his countenance suggested an underhanded mode of life. There was but one course: to suspend the man from the exercise of all priestly functions, and bid the smaller native priests take warning.

Father Vaillant had told the Bishop that he must by all means stop a night at Isleta, as he would like the priest there—Padre Jesus de Baca, an old white-haired man, almost blind, who had been at Isleta many years and had won the confidence and affection of his Indians.

When he approached this pueblo of Isleta, gleaming white across a low plain of grey sand, Father Latour's spirits rose. It was beautiful, that warm, rich whiteness of the church and the clustered town, shaded by a few bright acacia trees, with their intense blue-green like the colour of old paper window-blinds. That tree always awakened pleasant memories, recalling a garden in the south of France where he used to visit young cousins. As he rode up to the church, the old priest came out to meet him, and after his salutation stood looking at Father Latour, shading his failing eyes with his hand.

"And can this be my Bishop? So young a man?" he exclaimed.

They went into the priest's house by way of a garden, walled in behind the church. This enclosure was full of domesticated cactus plants, of many varieties and great size (it seemed the Padre loved them), and among these hung wicker cages made of willow twigs, full of parrots. There were even parrots hopping about the sanded paths—with one wing clipped to keep them at home. Father Jesus explained that parrot feathers were much prized by his Indians as ornaments for their ceremonial robes, and he had long ago found he could please his parishioners by raising the birds.

The priest's house was white within and without, like all the Isleta houses, and was almost as bare as an Indian dwelling. The old man was poor, and too soft-hearted to press the pueblo people for pesos. An Indian girl cooked his beans and cornmeal mush for him, he required little else. The girl was not very skilful, he said, but she was clean about her cooking. When the Bishop remarked that everything in this pueblo, even the streets, seemed clean, the Padre told him that near Isleta there was a hill of some white mineral, which the Indians ground up and used as whitewash. They had done this from time immemorial, and the village had always been noted for its whiteness. A little talk with Father Jesus revealed that he was simple almost to childishness, and very superstitious. But there was a quality of golden goodness about him. His right eye was overgrown by a cataract, and he kept his head tilted as if he were trying to see around it. All his movements were to the left, as if he were reaching or walking about some obstacle in his path.

After coming to the house by way of a garden full of parrots, Father Latour was amused to find that the sole ornament in the Padre's poor, bare little *sala*, was a wooden parrot, perched in a hoop and hung from one of the roof-logs. While Father Jesus was instructing his Indian girl in the kitchen, the Bishop took this carving down from its perch to examine it. It was cut from a single stick of wood, exactly the size of a living bird, body and tail rigid and straight, the head a little turned. The wings and tail and neck feathers were just indicated by the tool, and thinly painted. He was surprised to feel how light it was; the surface had the whiteness and velvety smoothness of very old wood. Though scarcely carved at all, merely smoothed into shape, it was strangely lifelike; a wooden pattern of parrots, as it were.

The Padre smiled when he found the Bishop with the bird in his hand.

"I see you have found my treasure! That, your Grace, is probably the oldest thing in the pueblo—older than the pueblo itself."

The parrot, Father Jesus said, had always been the bird of wonder and desire to the pueblo Indians. In ancient times its feathers were more valued than wampum and turquoises. Even before the Spaniards came, the pueblos of northern New Mexico used to send explorers along the dangerous and difficult trade routes down into tropical Mexico to bring back upon their bodies a cargo of parrot feathers. To purchase these the trader carried pouches full of turquoises from the Cerrillos hills near Santa Fé. When, very rarely, a trader succeeded in bringing back a live bird to his people, it was paid divine honours, and its death threw the whole village into the deepest gloom. Even the bones were piously preserved. There was in Isleta a parrot skull of great antiquity. His wooden bird he had bought from an old man who was much indebted to him, and who was about to die without descendants. Father Jesus had had his eye upon the bird for years. The Indian told him that his ancestors, generations ago, had brought it with them from the mother pueblo. The priest fondly believed that it was a portrait, done from life, of one of those rare birds that in ancient times were carried up alive, all the long trail of the tropics.

Father Jesus gave a good report of the Indians at Laguna and Ácoma. He used to go to those pueblos to hold services when he was younger, and had always found them friendly.

"At Ácoma," he said, "you can see something very holy. They have there a portrait of St. Joseph sent to them by one of the Kings of Spain, long ago, and it has worked many miracles. If the season is dry, the Ácoma people take the picture down to their farms at Acomita, and it never fails to produce rain. They have rain when none falls in all the country, and they have crops when the Laguna Indians have none."

2
Jacinto

Taking leave of Isleta and its priest early in the morning, Father Latour and his guide rode all day through the desert plain west of Albuquerque. It was like a country of dry ashes; no juniper, no rabbit brush, nothing but thickets of withered, dead-looking cactus, and patches of wild pumpkin—the only vegetation that had any vitality. It is a vine, remarkable for its tendency, not to spread and ramble, but to mass and mount. Its long, sharp, arrow-shaped leaves, frosted over with prickly silver, are thrust upward and crowded together; the whole rigid, up-thrust matted clump looks less like a plant than like a great colony of grey-green lizards, moving and suddenly arrested by fear.

As the morning wore on they had to make their way through a sand-storm which quite obscured the sun. Jacinto knew the country well, having crossed it often to go to the religious dances at Laguna, but he rode with his head low and a purple handkerchief tied over his mouth. Coming from a pueblo among woods and water, he had a poor opinion of this plain. At noon he alighted and collected enough greasewood to boil the Bishop's coffee. They knelt on either side of the fire, the sand curling about them so that the bread became gritty as they ate it.

The sun set red in an atmosphere murky with sand. The travellers made a dry camp and rolled themselves in their blankets. All night a cold wind blew over them. Father Latour was so stiff that he arose long before daybreak. The dawn came at last, fair and clear, and they made an early start.

About the middle of that afternoon Jacinto pointed out Laguna in the distance, lying, apparently, in the midst of bright yellow waves of high sand dunes—yellow as ochre. As they approached, Father Latour found these were petrified sand dunes; long waves of soft, gritty yellow rock, shining and bare except for a few lines of dark juniper that grew out of the weather cracks,—little trees, and very, very old. At the foot of this sweep of rock waves was the blue lake, a stone basin full of water, from which the pueblo took its name.

The kindly Padre at Isleta had sent his cook's brother off on foot to warn the Laguna people that the new High Priest was coming, and that he was a good man and did not want money. They were prepared accordingly; the church was clean and the doors were open; a small white church, painted above and about the altar with gods of wind and rain and thunder, sun and moon, linked together in a geometrical design of crimson and blue and dark green, so that the end of the church seemed to be hung with tapestry. It recalled to Father Latour the interior of a Persian chieftain's tent he had seen in a textile exhibit at Lyons. Whether this decoration had been done by Spanish missionaries or by Indian converts, he was unable to find out.

The Governor told him that his people would come to Mass in the morning, and that there were a number of children to be baptized. He offered the Bishop the sacristy for the night, but there was a damp, earthy smell about that chamber, and Father Latour had already made up his mind that he would like to sleep on the rock dunes, under the junipers.

Jacinto got firewood and good water from the Lagunas, and they made their camp in a pleasant spot on the rocks north of the village. As the sun dropped low, the light brought the white church and the yellow adobe houses up into relief from the flat ledges. Behind their camp, not far away, lay a group of great mesas. The Bishop asked Jacinto if he knew the name of the one nearest them.

"No, I not know any name," he shook his head. "I know Indian name," he added, as if, for once, he were thinking aloud.

"And what is the Indian name?"

"The Laguna Indians call Snow-Bird mountain." He spoke somewhat unwillingly.

"That is very nice," said the Bishop musingly. "Yes, that is a pretty name."

"Oh, Indians have nice names too!" Jacinto replied quickly, with a curl of the lip. Then, as if he felt he had taken out on the Bishop a reproach not deserved, he said in a moment: "The Laguna people think it very funny for a big priest to be a young man. The Governor say, how can I call him Padre when he is younger than my sons?"

There was a note of pride in Jacinto's voice very flattering to the Bishop. He had noticed how kind the Indian voice could be when it was kind at all; a slight inflection made one feel that one had received a great compliment.

"I am not very young in heart, Jacinto. How old are you, my boy?"

"Twenty-six."

"Have you a son?"

"One. Baby. Not very long born."

Jacinto usually dropped the article in speaking Spanish, just as he did in speaking English, though the Bishop had noticed that when he did give a noun its article, he used the right one. The customary omission, therefore, seemed to be a matter of taste, not ignorance. In the Indian conception of language, such attachments were superfluous and unpleasing, perhaps.

They relapsed into the silence which was their usual form of intercourse. The Bishop sat drinking his coffee slowly out of the tin cup, keeping the pot near the embers. The sun had set now, the yellow rocks were turning grey, down in the pueblo the light of the cook fires made red patches of the glassless windows, and the smell of piñon smoke came softly through the still air. The whole western sky was the colour of golden ashes, with here and there a flush of red on the lip of a little cloud. High above the horizon the evening-star flickered like a lamp just lit, and close beside it was another star of constant light, much smaller.

Jacinto threw away the end of his cornhusk cigarette and again spoke without being addressed.

"The ev-en-ing-star," he said in English, slowly and somewhat sententiously, then relapsed into Spanish. "You see the little star beside, Padre? Indians call him the guide."

The two companions sat, each thinking his own thoughts as night closed in about them; a blue night set with stars, the bulk of the solitary mesas cutting into the firmament. The Bishop seldom questioned Jacinto about his thoughts or beliefs. He didn't think it polite, and he believed it to be useless. There was no way in which he could transfer his own memories of European civilization into the Indian mind, and he was quite willing to believe that behind Jacinto there was a long tradition, a story of experience, which no language could translate to him. A chill came with the darkness. Father Latour put on his old fur-lined cloak, and Jacinto, loosening the blanket tied about his loins, drew it up over his head and shoulders.

"Many stars," he said presently. "What you think about the stars, Padre?"

"The wise men tell us they are worlds, like ours, Jacinto."

The end of the Indian's cigarette grew bright and then dull again before he spoke. "I think not," he said in the tone of one who has considered a proposition fairly and rejected it. "I think they are leaders—great spirits."

"Perhaps they are," said the Bishop with a sigh. "Whatever they are, they are great. Let us say *Our Father,* and go to sleep, my boy."

Kneeling on either side of the embers they repeated the prayer together and then rolled up in their blankets. The Bishop went to sleep thinking with satisfaction that he was beginning to have some sort of human companionship with his Indian boy. One called the young Indians "boys," perhaps because there was something youthful and elastic in their bodies. Certainly about their behaviour there was nothing boyish in the American sense, nor even in the European sense. Jacinto was never, by any chance, naïf; he was never taken by surprise. One felt that his training, whatever it had been, had prepared him to meet any situation which might confront him. He was as much at home in the Bishop's study as in his own pueblo—and he was never too much at home anywhere. Father Latour felt he had gone a good way toward gaining his guide's friendship, though he did not know how.

The truth was, Jacinto liked the Bishop's way of meeting people; thought he had the right tone with Padre Gallegos, the right tone with Padre Jesus, and that he had good manners with the Indians. In his experience, white people, when they addressed Indians, always put on a false face. There were many kinds of false faces; Father Vaillant's, for example, was kindly but too vehement. The Bishop put on none at all. He stood straight and turned to the Governor of Laguna, and his face underwent no change. Jacinto thought this remarkable.

3
The Rock

After early Mass the next morning Father Latour and his guide rode off across the low plain that lies between Laguna and Ácoma. In all his travels the Bishop had seen no country like this. From the flat red sea of sand rose great rock mesas, generally Gothic in outline, resembling vast cathedrals. They were not crowded together in disorder, but placed in wide spaces, long vistas between. This plain might once have been an enormous city, all the smaller quarters destroyed by time, only the public buildings left,—piles of architecture that were like mountains. The sandy soil of the plain had a light sprinkling of junipers, and was splotched with masses of blooming rabbit brush,—that olive-coloured plant that grows in high waves like a tossing sea, at this season covered with a thatch of bloom, yellow as gorse, or orange like marigolds.

This mesa plain had an appearance of great antiquity, and of incompleteness; as if, with all the materials for world-making assembled, the Creator had desisted, gone away and left everything on the point of being brought together, on the eve of being arranged into mountain, plain, plateau. The country was still waiting to be made into a landscape.

Ever afterward the Bishop remembered his first ride to Ácoma as his introduction to the mesa country. One thing which struck him at once was that every mesa was duplicated by a cloud mesa, like a reflection, which lay motionless above it or moved slowly up from behind it. These cloud formations seemed to be always there, however hot and blue the sky. Sometimes they were flat terraces, ledges of vapour; sometimes they were dome-shaped, or fantastic, like the tops of silvery pagodas, rising one above another, as if an oriental city lay directly behind the rock. The great tables of granite set down in an empty plain were inconceivable without their attendant clouds, which were a part of them, as the smoke is part of the censer, or the foam of the wave.

Coming along the Santa Fé trail, in the vast plains of Kansas, Father Latour had found the sky more a desert than the land; a hard, empty blue, very monotonous to the eyes of a Frenchman. But west of the Pecos all that changed; here there was always activity overhead, clouds forming and moving all day long. Whether they were dark and full of violence, or soft and white with luxurious idleness, they powerfully affected the world beneath them. The desert, the mountains and mesas, were continually re-formed and re-coloured by the cloud shadows. The whole country seemed fluid to the eye under this constant change of accent, this ever-varying distribution of light.

Jacinto interrupted these reflections by an exclamation.

"Ácoma!" He stopped his mule.

The Bishop, following with his eye the straight, pointing Indian hand, saw, far away, two great mesas. They were almost square in shape, and at this distance seemed close together, though they were really some miles apart.

"The far one"—his guide still pointed.

The Bishop's eyes were not so sharp as Jacinto's, but now, looking down upon the top of the farther mesa from the high land on which they halted, he saw a flat white outline on the grey surface—a white square made up of squares. That, his guide said, was the pueblo of Ácoma.

Riding on, they presently drew rein under the Enchanted Mesa, and Jacinto told him that on this, too, there had once been a village, but the stairway which had been the only access to it was broken off by a great storm many centuries ago, and its people had perished up there from hunger.

But how, the Bishop asked him, did men first think of living on top of naked rocks like these, hundreds of feet in the air, without soil or water?

Jacinto shrugged. "A man can do whole lot when they hunt him day and night like an animal. Navajos on the north, Apaches on the south; the Ácoma run up a rock to be safe."

All this plain, the Bishop gathered, had once been the scene of a periodic man-hunt; these Indians, born in fear and dying by violence for generations, had at last taken this leap away from the earth, and on that rock had found the hope of all suffering and tormented creatures—safety. They came down to the plain to hunt and to grow their crops, but there was always a place to go back to. If a band of Navajos were on the Ácoma's trail, there was still one hope; if he could reach his rock—Sanctuary! On the winding stone stairway up the cliff, a handful of men could keep off a multitude. The rock of Ácoma had never been taken by a foe but once,—by Spaniards in armour. It was very different from a mountain fastness; more lonely, more stark and grim, more appealing to the imagination. The rock, when one came to think of it, was the utmost expression of human need; even mere feeling yearned for it; it was the highest comparison of loyalty in love and friendship. Christ Himself had used that comparison for the disciple to whom He gave the keys of His Church. And the Hebrews of the Old Testament, always being carried captive into foreign lands,—their rock was an idea of God, the only thing their conquerors could not take from them.

Already the Bishop had observed in Indian life a strange literalness, often shocking and disconcerting. The Ácomas, who must share the universal human yearning for something permanent, enduring, without shadow of change,—they had their idea in substance. They actually lived upon their Rock; were born upon it and died upon it. There was an element of exaggeration in anything so simple!

As they drew near the Ácoma mesa, dark clouds began boiling up from behind it, like ink spots spreading in a brilliant sky.

"Rain come," remarked Jacinto. "That is good. They will be well disposed." He left the mules in a stake corral at the foot of the mesa, took up the blankets, and hurried Father Latour into the narrow crack in the rock where the craggy edges formed a kind of natural stairway up the cliff. Wherever the footing was treacherous, it was helped out by little hand-holds, ground into the stone like smooth mittens. The mesa was absolutely naked of vegetation, but at its foot a rank plant grew conspicuously out of the sand; a plant with big white blossoms like Easter lilies. By its dark blue-green leaves, large and coarse-toothed, Father Latour recognized a species of the noxious datura. The size and luxuriance of these nightshades astonished him. They looked like great artificial plants, made of shining silk.

While they were ascending the rock, deafening thunder broke over their heads, and the rain began to fall as if it were spilled from a cloud-burst. Drawing into a deep twist of the stairway, under an overhanging ledge, they watched the water shaken in heavy curtains in the air before them. In a moment the seam in which they stood was like the channel of a brook. Looking out over the great plain spotted with mesas and glittering with rain sheets, the Bishop saw the distant mountains bright with sunlight. Again he thought that the first Creation morning might have looked like this, when the dry land was first drawn up out of the deep, and all was confusion.

The storm was over in half an hour. By the time the Bishop and his guide reached the last turn in the trail, and rose through the crack, stepping out on the flat top of the rock, the noontide sun was blazing down upon Ácoma with almost insupportable brightness. The bare stone floor of the town and its deep-worn paths were washed white and clean, and those depressions in the surface which the Ácomas call their cisterns, were full of fresh rain water. Already the women were bringing out their clothes, to begin washing. The drinking water was carried up the stairway in earthen jars on the heads of the women, from a secret spring below; but for all other purposes the people depended on the rainfall held in these cisterns.

The top of the mesa was about ten acres in extent, the Bishop judged, and there was not a tree or a blade of green upon it; not a handful of soil, except the churchyard, held in by an adobe wall, where the earth for burial had been carried up in baskets from the plain below. The white dwellings, two and three storeyed, were not scattered, but huddled together in a close cluster, with no protecting slope of ground or shoulder of rock, lying flat against the flat, bright against the bright,—both the rock and the plastered houses threw off the sun glare blindingly.

At the very edge of the mesa, overhanging the abyss so that its retaining wall was like a part of the cliff itself, was the old warlike church of Ácoma, with its two stone towers. Gaunt, grim, grey, its nave rising some seventy feet to a sagging, half-ruined roof, it was more like a fortress than a place of worship. That spacious interior depressed the Bishop as no other mission church had done. He held a service there before midday, and he had never found it so hard to go through the ceremony of the Mass. Before him, on the grey floor, in the grey light, a group of bright shawls and blankets, some fifty or sixty silent faces; above and behind them the grey walls. He felt as if he were celebrating Mass at the bottom of the sea, for antediluvian creatures; for types of life so old, so hardened, so shut within their shells, that the sacrifice on Calvary could hardly reach back so far. Those shell-like backs behind him might be saved by baptism and divine grace, as undeveloped infants are, but hardly through any experience of their own, he thought. When he blessed them and sent them away, it was with a sense of inadequacy and spiritual defeat.

After he had laid aside his vestments, Father Latour went over the church with Jacinto. As he examined it his wonder grew. What need had there ever been for this great church at Ácoma? It was built early in sixteen hundred, by Fray Juan Ramirez, a great missionary, who laboured on the Rock of Ácoma for twenty years or more. It was Father Ramirez, too, who made the mule trail down the other side,—the only path by which a burro can ascend the mesa, and which is still called "El Camino del Padre."

The more Father Latour examined this church, the more he was inclined to think that Fray Ramirez, or some Spanish priest who followed him, was not altogether innocent of worldly ambition, and that they built for their own satisfaction, perhaps, rather than according to the needs of the Indians. The magnificent site, the natural grandeur of this stronghold, might well have turned their heads a little. Powerful men they must have been, those Spanish Fathers, to draft Indian labour for this great work without military support. Every stone in that structure, every handful of earth in those many thousand pounds of adobe, was carried up the trail on the backs of men and boys and women. And the great carved beams of the roof—Father Latour looked at them with amazement. In all the plain through which he had come he had seen no trees but a few stunted piñons. He asked Jacinto where these huge timbers could have been found.

"San Mateo mountain, I guess."

"But the San Mateo mountains must be forty or fifty miles away. How could they bring such timbers?"

Jacinto shrugged. "Ácomas carry." Certainly there was no other explanation.

Besides the church proper there was the cloister, large, thick-walled, which must have required an enormous labour of portage from the plain. The deep cloister corridors were cool when the rock outside was blistering; the low arches opened on an enclosed garden which, judging from its depth of earth, must once have been very verdant. Pacing those shady passages, with four feet of solid, windowless adobe shutting out everything but the green garden and the turquoise sky above, the early missionaries might well have forgotten the poor Ácomas, that tribe of ancient rock-turtles, and believed themselves in some cloister hung on a spur of the Pyrenees.

In the grey dust of the enclosed garden two thin, half-dead peach trees still struggled with the drouth, the kind of unlikely tree that grows up from an old root and never bears. By the wall yellow suckers put out from an old vine stump, very thick and hard, which must once have borne its ripe clusters.

Built upon the north-east corner of the cloister the Bishop found a loggia—roofed, but with open sides, looking down on the white pueblo and the tawny rock, and over the wide plain below. There he decided he would spend the night. From this loggia he watched the sun go down; watched the desert become dark, the shadows creep upward. Abroad in the plain the scattered mesa tops, red with the afterglow, one by one lost their light, like candles going out. He was on a naked rock in the desert, in the stone age, a prey to homesickness for his own kind, his own epoch, for European man and his glorious history of desire and dreams. Through all the centuries that his own part of the world had been changing like the sky at daybreak, this people had been fixed, increasing neither in numbers nor desires, rock-turtles on their rock. Something reptilian he felt here, something that had endured by immobility, a kind of life out of reach, like the crustaceans in their armour.

On his homeward way the Bishop spent another night with Father Jesus, the good priest at Isleta, who talked with him much of the Moqui country and of those very old rock-set pueblos still farther to the west. One story related to a long-forgotten friar at Ácoma, and was somewhat as follows:

4
The Legend of Fray Baltazar

Some time in the very early years of seventeen hundred, nearly fifty years after the great Indian uprising in which all the missionaries and all the Spaniards in northern new Mexico were either driven out or murdered, after the country had been reconquered and new missionaries had come to take the place of the martyrs, a certain Friar Baltazar Montoya was priest of Ácoma. He was of a tyrannical and overbearing disposition and bore a hard hand on the natives. All the missions now in ruins were active then, each had its resident priest, who lived for the people or upon the people, according to his nature. Friar Baltazar was one of the most ambitious and exacting. It was his belief that the pueblo of Ácoma existed chiefly to support its fine church, and that this should be the pride of the Indians as it was his. He took the best of their corn and beans and squashes for his table, and selected the choicest portions when they slaughtered a sheep, chose their best hides to carpet his dwelling. Moreover, he exacted a heavy tribute in labour. He was never done with having earth carried up from the plain in baskets. He enlarged the churchyard and made the deep garden in the cloister, enriching it with dung from the corrals. Here he was able to grow a wonderful garden, since it was watered every evening by women,—and this despite the fact that it was not proper that a woman should ever enter the cloister at all. Each woman owed the Padre so many *ollas* of water a week from the cisterns, and they murmured not only because of the labour, but because of the drain on their water-supply.

Baltazar was not a lazy man, and in his first years there, before he became stout, he made long journeys in behalf of his mission and his garden. He went as far as Oraibi, many days' journey, to select their best peach seeds. (The peach orchards of Oraibi were very old, having been cultivated since the days of the earliest Spanish expeditions, when Coronado's captains gave the Moquis peach seeds brought from Spain.) His grape cuttings were brought from Sonora in baskets on muleback, and he would go all the way to the Villa (Santa Fé) for choice garden seeds, at the season when pack trains came up the Rio Grande valley. The early churchmen did a great business in carrying seeds about, though the Indians and Mexicans were satisfied with beans and squashes and chili, asking nothing more.

Friar Baltazar was from a religious house in Spain which was noted for good living, and he himself had worked in the refectory. He was an excellent cook and something of a carpenter, and he took a great deal of trouble to make himself comfortable upon that rock at the end of the world. He drafted two Indian boys into his service, one to care for his ass and work in the garden, the other to cook and wait upon him at table. In time, as he grew more unwieldy in figure, he adopted a third boy and employed him as a runner to the distant missions. This boy would go on foot all the way to the Villa for red cloth or an iron spade or a new knife, stopping at Bernalillo to bring home a wineskin full of grape brandy. He would go five days' journey to the Sandia mountains to catch fish and dry or salt them for the Padre's fast-days, or run to Zuñi, where the Fathers raised rabbits, and bring back a pair for the spit. His errands were seldom of an ecclesiastical nature.

It was clear that the Friar at Ácoma lived more after the flesh than after the spirit. The difficulty of obtaining an interesting and varied diet on a naked rock seemed only to whet his appetite and tempt his resourcefulness. But his sensuality went no further than his garden and table. Carnal commerce with the Indian women would have been very easy indeed, and the Friar was at the hardy age of ripe manhood when such temptations are peculiarly sharp. But the missionaries had early discovered that the slightest departure from chastity greatly weakened their influence and authority with their Indian converts. The Indians themselves sometimes practised continence as a penance, or as a strong medicine with the spirits, and they were very willing that their Padre should practise it for them. The consequences of carnal indulgence were perhaps more serious here than in Spain, and Friar Baltazar seems never to have given his flock an opportunity to exult over his frailty.

He held his seat at Ácoma for nearly fifteen prosperous years, constantly improving his church and his living-quarters, growing new vegetables and medicinal herbs, making soap from the yucca root. Even after he became stout, his arms were strong and muscular, his fingers clever. He cultivated his peach trees, and watched over his garden like a little kingdom, never allowing the native women to grow slack in the water-supply. His first serving-boys were released to marry, and others succeeded them, who were even more minutely trained.

Baltazar's tyranny grew little by little, and the Ácoma people were sometimes at the point of revolt. But they could not estimate just how powerful the Padre's magic might be and were afraid to put it to the test. There was no doubt that the holy picture of St. Joseph had come to them from the King of Spain by the request of this Padre, and that picture had been more effective in averting drouth than all the native rain-makers had been. Properly entreated and honoured, the painting had never failed to produce rain. Ácoma had not lost its crops since Friar Baltazar first brought the picture to them, though at Laguna and Zuñi there had been drouths that compelled the people to live upon their famine store,—an alarming extremity.

The Laguna Indians were constantly sending legations to Ácoma to negotiate terms at which they could rent the holy picture, but Friar Baltazar had warned them never to let it go. If such powerful protection were withdrawn, or if the Padre should turn the magic against them, the consequences might be disastrous to the pueblo. Better give him his choice of grain and lambs and pottery, and allow him his three serving-boys. So the missionary and his converts rubbed along in seeming friendliness.

One summer the Friar, who did not make long journeys now that he had grown large in girth, decided that he would like company,—someone to admire his fine garden, his ingenious kitchen, his airy loggia with its rugs and water jars, where he meditated and took his after-dinner siesta. So he planned to give a dinner party in the week after St. John's Day.

He sent his runner to Zuñi, Laguna, Isleta, and bade the Padres to a feast. They came upon the day, four of them, for there were two priests at Zuñi. The stable-boy was stationed at the foot of the rock to take their beasts and conduct the visitors up the stairway. At the head of the trail Baltazar received them. They were shown over the place, and spent the morning gossiping in the cloister walks, cool and silent, though the naked rock outside was almost too hot for the hand to touch. The vine leaves rustled agreeably in the breeze, and the earth about the carrot and onion tops, as it dried from last night's watering, gave off a pleasant smell. The guests thought their host lived very well, and they wished they had his secret. If he was a trifle boastful of his air-bound seat, no one could blame him.

With the dinner, Baltazar had taken extravagant pains. The monastery in which he had learned to cook was off the main highway to Seville; the Spanish nobles and the King himself sometimes stopped there for entertainment. In that great kitchen, with its multiplicity of spits, small enough to roast a lark and large enough to roast a boar, the Friar had learned a thing or two about sauces, and in his lonely years at Ácoma he had bettered his instruction by a natural aptitude for the art. The poverty of materials had proved an incentive rather than a discouragement.

Certainly the visiting missionaries had never sat down to food like that which rejoiced them to-day in the cool refectory, the blinds open just enough to admit a streak of throbbing desert far below them. Their host was telling them pompously that he would have a fountain in the cloister close when they came again. He had to check his hungry guests in their zeal for the relishes and the soup, warning them to save their mettle for what was to come. The roast was to be a wild turkey, superbly done—but that, alas, was never tasted. The course which preceded it was the host's especial care, and here he had trusted nothing to his cook; hare *jardinière* (his carrots and onions were tender and well flavoured), with a sauce which he had been perfecting for many years. This entrée was brought from the kitchen in a large earthen dish—but not large enough, for with its luxury of sauce and floating carrots it filled the platter to the brim. The stable-boy was serving to-day, as the cook could not leave his spits, and he had been neat, brisk, and efficient. The Friar was pleased with him, and was wondering whether he could not find some little medal of bronze or silver-gilt to reward him for his pains.

When the hare in its sauce came on, the priest from Isleta chanced to be telling a funny story at which the company were laughing uproariously. The serving-boy, who knew a little Spanish, was apparently trying to get the point of the recital which made the Padres so merry. At any rate, he became distracted, and as he passed behind the senior priest of Zuñi, he tipped his full platter and spilled a stream of rich brown gravy over the good man's head and shoulders. Baltazar was quick-tempered, and he had been drinking freely of the fiery grape brandy. He caught up the empty pewter mug at his right and threw it at the clumsy lad with a malediction. It struck the boy on the side of the head. He dropped the platter, staggered a few steps, and fell down. He did not get up, nor did he move. The Padre from Zuñi was skilled in medicine. Wiping the sauce from his eyes, he bent over the boy and examined him.

"*Muerto*," he whispered. With that he plucked his junior priest by the sleeve, and the two bolted across the garden without another word and made for the head of the stairway. In a moment the Padres of Laguna and Isleta unceremoniously followed their example. With remarkable speed the four guests got them down from the rock, saddled their mules, and urged them across the plain.

Baltazar was left alone with the consequences of his haste. Unfortunately the cook, astonished at the prolonged silence, had looked in at the door just as the last pair of brown gowns were vanishing across the cloister. He saw his comrade lying upon the floor, and silently disappeared from the premises by an exit known only to himself.

When Friar Baltazar went into the kitchen he found it solitary, the turkey still dripping on the spit. Certainly he had no appetite for the roast. He felt, indeed, very remorseful and uncomfortable, also indignant with his departed guests. For a moment he entertained the idea of following them; but a temporary flight would only weaken his position, and a permanent evacuation was not to be thought of. His garden was at its prime, his peaches were just coming ripe, and his vines hung heavy with green clusters. Mechanically he took the turkey from the spit, not because he felt any inclination for food, but from an instinct of compassion, quite as if the bird could suffer from being burned to a crisp. This done, he repaired to his loggia and sat down to read his breviary, which he had neglected for several days, having been so occupied in the refectory. He had begrudged no pains to that sauce which had been his undoing.

The airy loggia, where he customarily took his afternoon repose, was like a birdcage hung in the breeze. Through its open archways he looked down on the huddled pueblo, and out over the great mesa-strewn plain far below. He was unable to fix his mind upon his office. The pueblo down there was much too quiet. At this hour there should be a few women washing pots or rags, a few children playing by the cisterns and chasing the turkeys. But to-day the rock top baked in the fire of the sun in utter silence, not one human being was visible—yes, one, though he had not been there a moment ago. At the head of the stone stairway, there was a patch of lustrous black, just above the rocks; and Indian's hair. They had set a guard at the trail head.

Now the Padre began to feel alarmed, to wish he had gone down that stairway with the others, while there was yet time. He wished he were anywhere in the world but on this rock. There was old Father Ramirez's donkey path; but if the Indians were watching one road, they would watch the other. The spot of black hair never stirred; and there were but those two ways down to the plain, only those. . . . Whichever way one turned, three hundred and fifty feet of naked cliff, without one tree or shrub a man could cling to.

As the sun sank lower and lower, there began a deep, singing murmur of male voices from the pueblo below him, not a chant, but the rhythmical intonation of Indian oratory when a serious matter is under discussion. Frightful stories of the torture of the missionaries in the great rebellion of 1680 flashed into Friar Baltazar's mind; how one Franciscan had his eyes torn out, another had been burned, and the old Padre at Jamez had been stripped naked and driven on all fours about the plaza all night, with drunken Indians straddling his back, until he rolled over dead from exhaustion.

Moonrise from the loggia was an impressive sight, even to this Brother who was not over-impressionable. But to-night he wished he could keep the moon from coming up through the floor of the desert,—the moon was the clock which began things in the pueblo. He watched with horror for that golden rim against the deep blue velvet of the night.

The moon came, and at its coming the Ácoma people issued from their doors. A company of men walked silently across the rock to the cloister. They came up the ladder and appeared in the loggia. The Friar asked them gruffly what they wanted, but they made no reply. Not once speaking to him or to each other, they bound his feet together and tied his arms to his sides.

The Ácoma people told afterwards that he did not supplicate or struggle; had he done so, they might have dealt more cruelly with him. But he knew his Indians, and that when once they had collectively made up their pueblo mind . . . Moreover, he was a proud old Spaniard, and had a certain fortitude lodged in his well-nourished body. He was accustomed to command, not to entreat, and he retained the respect of his Indian vassals to the end.

They carried him down the ladder and through the cloister and across the rock to the most precipitous cliff—the one over which the Ácoma women flung broken pots and such refuse as the turkeys would not eat. There the people were assembled. They cut his bonds, and taking him by the hands and feet, swung him out over the rock-edge and back a few times. He was heavy, and perhaps they thought this dangerous sport. No sound but hissing breath came through his teeth. The four executioners took him up again from the brink where they had laid him, and, after a few feints, dropped him in mid-air.

So did they rid their rock of their tyrant, whom on the whole they had liked very well. But everything has its day. The execution was not followed by any sacrilege to the church or defiling of holy vessels, but merely by a division of the Padre's stores and household goods. The women, indeed, took pleasure in watching the garden pine and waste away from thirst, and ventured into the cloisters to laugh and chatter at the whitening foliage of the peach trees, and the green grapes shrivelling on the vines.

When the next priest came, years afterward, he found no ill will awaiting him. He was a native Mexican, of unpretentious tastes, who was well satisfied with beans and jerked meat, and let the pueblo turkey flock scratch in the hot dust that had once been Baltazar's garden. The old peach stumps kept sending up pale sprouts for many years.

BOOK FOUR

Snake Root

1
The Night at Pecos

A month after the Bishop's visit to Albuquerque and Ácoma, the genial Father Gallegos was formally suspended, and Father Vaillant himself took charge of the parish. At first there was bitter feeling; the rich *rancheros* and the merry ladies of Albuquerque were very hostile to the French priest. He began his reforms at once. Everything was changed. The holy-days, which had been occasions of revelry under Padre Gallegos, were now days of austere devotion. The fickle Mexican population soon found as much diversion in being devout as they had once found in being scandalous. Father Vaillant wrote to his sister Philomène, in France, that the temper of his parish was like that of a boys' school; under one master the lads try to excel one another in mischief and disobedience, under another they vie with each other in acts of loyalty. The Novena preceding Christmas, which had long been celebrated by dances and hilarious merrymaking, was this year a great revival of religious zeal.

Though Father Vaillant had all the duties of a parish priest at Albuquerque, he was still Vicar General, and in February the Bishop dispatched him on urgent business to Las Vegas. He did not return on the day that he was expected, and when several days passed with no word from him, Father Latour began to feel some anxiety.

One morning at day-break a very sick Indian boy rode into the Bishop's court-yard on Father Joseph's white mule, Contento, bringing bad news. The Padre, he said, had stopped at his village in the Pecos mountains where black measles had broken out, to give the sacrament to the dying, and had fallen ill of the sickness. The boy himself had been well when he started for Santa Fé, but had become sick on the way.

The Bishop had the messenger put into the woodhouse, an isolated building at the end of the garden, where the Sisters of Loretto could tend him. He instructed the Mother Superior to pack a bag with such medicines and comforts for the sick as he could carry, and told Fructosa, his cook, to put up for him the provisions he usually took on horseback journeys. When his man brought a pack-mule and his own mule, Angelica, to the door, Father Latour, already in his rough riding-breeches and buckskin jacket, looked at the handsome beast and shook his head.

"No, leave her with Contento. The new army mule is heavier, and will do for this journey."

The Bishop rode out of Santa Fé two hours after the Indian messenger rode in. He was going direct to the pueblo of Pecos, where he would pick up Jacinto. It was late in the afternoon when he reached the pueblo, lying low on its red rock ledges, half-surrounded by a crown of fir-clad mountains, and facing a sea of junipers and cedars. The Bishop had meant to get fresh horses at Pecos and push on through the mountains, but Jacinto and the older Indians who gathered about the horseman strongly advised him to spend the night there and start in the early morning. The sun was shining brilliantly in a blue sky, but in the west, behind the mountain, lay a great stationary black cloud, opaque and motionless as a ledge of rock. The old men looked at it and shook their heads.

"Very big wind," said the governor gravely.

Unwillingly the Bishop dismounted and gave his mules to Jacinto; it seemed to him that he was wasting time. There was still an hour before nightfall, and he spent that hour pacing up and down the crust of bare rock between the village and the ruin of the old mission church. The sun was sinking, a red ball which threw a copper glow over the pine-covered ridge of mountains, and edged that inky, ominous cloud with molten silver. The great red earth walls of the mission, red as brick-dust, yawned gloomily before him,—part of the roof had fallen in, and the rest would soon go.

At this moment Father Joseph was lying dangerously ill in the dirt and discomfort of an Indian village in winter. Why, the Bishop was asking himself, had he ever brought his friend to this life of hardship and danger? Father Vaillant had been frail from childhood, though he had the endurance resulting from exhaustless enthusiasm. The Brothers at Montferrand were not given to coddling boys, but every year they used to send this one away for a rest in the high Volvic mountains, because his vitality ran down under the confinement of college life. Twice, while he and Father Latour were missionaries in Ohio, Joseph had been at death's door; once so ill with cholera that the newspapers had printed his name in the death list. On that occasion their Ohio Bishop had christened him *Trompe-la-Mort*. Yes, Father Latour told himself, *Blanchet* had outwitted death so often, there was always the chance he would do it again.

Walking about the walls of the ruin, the Bishop discovered that the sacristy was dry and clean, and he decided to spend the night there, wrapped in his blankets, on one of the earthen benches that ran about the inner walls. While he was examining this room, the wind began to howl about the old church, and darkness fell quickly. From the low doorways of the pueblo ruddy fire-light was gleaming—singularly grateful to the eye. Waiting for him on the rocks, he recognized the slight figure of Jacinto, his blanket drawn close about his head, his shoulders bowed to the wind.

The young Indian said that supper was ready, and the Bishop followed him to his particular lair in those rows of little houses all alike and all built together. There was a ladder before Jacinto's door which led up to a second storey, but that was the dwelling of another family; the roof of Jacinto's house made a veranda for the family above him. The Bishop bent his head under the low doorway and stepped down; the floor of the room was a long step below the door-sill—the Indian way of preventing drafts. The room into which he descended was long and narrow, smoothly whitewashed, and clean, to the eye, at least, because of its very bareness. There was nothing on the walls but a few fox pelts and strings of gourds and red peppers. The richly coloured blankets of which Jacinto was very proud were folded in piles on the earth settle,—it was there he and his wife slept, near the fireplace. The earth of that settle became warm during the day and held its heat until morning, like the Russian peasants' stove-bed. Over the fire a pot of beans and dried meat was simmering. The burning piñon logs filled the room with sweet-smelling smoke. Clara, Jacinto's wife, smiled at the priest as he entered. She ladled out the stew, and the Bishop and Jacinto sat down on the floor beside the fire, each with his bowl. Between them Clara put a basin full of hot corn-bread baked with squash seeds,—an Indian delicacy comparable to raisin bread among the whites. The Bishop said a blessing and broke the bread with his hands. While the two men ate, the young woman watched them and stirred a tiny cradle of deerskin which hung by thongs from the roof poles. Jacinto, when questioned, said sadly that the baby was ailing. Father Latour did not ask to see it; it would be swathed in layers of wrappings, he knew; even its face and head would be covered against drafts. Indian babies were never bathed in winter, and it was useless to suggest treatment for the sick ones. On that subject the Indian ear was closed to advice.

    It was a pity, too, that he could do nothing for Jacinto's baby. Cradles were not many in the pueblo of Pecos. The tribe was dying out; infant mortality was heavy, and the young couples did not reproduce freely,—the life-force seemed low. Smallpox and measles had taken heavy toll here time and again.

    Of course there were other explanations, credited by many good people in Santa Fé. Pecos had more than its share of dark legends,—perhaps that was because it had been too tempting to white men, and had had more than its share of history. It was said that this people had from time immemorial kept a ceremonial fire burning in some cave in the mountain, a fire that had never been allowed to go out, and had never been revealed to white men. The story was that the service of this fire sapped the strength of the young men appointed to serve it,—always the best of the tribe. Father Latour thought this hardly probable. Why should it be very arduous, in a mountain full of timber, to feed a fire so small that its whereabouts had been concealed for centuries?

There was also the snake story, reported by the early explorers, both Spanish and American, and believed ever since: that this tribe was peculiarly addicted to snake worship, that they kept rattlesnakes concealed in their houses, and somewhere in the mountain guarded an enormous serpent which they brought to the pueblo for certain feasts. It was said that they sacrificed young babies to the great snake, and thus diminished their numbers.

It seemed much more likely that the contagious diseases brought by white men were the real cause of the shrinkage of the tribe. Among the Indians, measles, scarlatina and whooping-cough were as deadly as typhus or cholera. Certainly, the tribe was decreasing every year. Jacinto's house was at one end of the living pueblo; behind it were long rock ridges of dead pueblo,—empty houses ruined by weather and now scarcely more than piles of earth and stone. The population of the living streets was less than one hundred adults.* This was all that was left of the rich and populous Cicuyè of Coronado's expedition. Then, by his report, there were six thousand souls in the Indian town. They had rich fields irrigated from the Pecos River. The streams were full of fish, the mountain was full of game. The pueblo, indeed, seemed to lie upon the knees of these verdant mountains, like a favoured child. Out yonder, on the juniper-spotted plateau in front of the village, the Spaniards had camped, exacting a heavy tribute of corn and furs and cotton garments from their hapless hosts. It was from here, the story went, that they set forth in the spring on their ill-fated search for the seven golden cities of Quivera, taking with them slaves and concubines ravished from the Pecos people.

As Father Latour sat by the fire and listened to the wind sweeping down from the mountains and howling over the plateau, he thought of these things; and he could not help wondering whether Jacinto, sitting silent by the same fire, was thinking of them, too. The wind, he knew, was blowing out of the inky cloud bank that lay behind the mountain at sunset; but it might well be blowing out of a remote, black past. The only human voice raised against it was the feeble wailing of the sick child in the cradle. Clara ate noiselessly in a corner, Jacinto looked into the fire.

The Bishop read his breviary by the fire-light for an hour. Then, warmed to the bone and assured that his roll of blankets was warmed through, he rose to go. Jacinto followed with the blankets and one of his own buffalo robes. They went along a line of red doorways and across the bare rock to the gaunt ruin, whose lateral walls, with their buttresses, still braved the storm and let in the starlight.

---

* In actual fact, the dying pueblo of Pecos was abandoned some years before the American occupation of New Mexico.

2
Stone Lips

It was not difficult for the Bishop to waken early. After midnight his body became more and more chilled and cramped. He said his prayers before he rolled out of his blankets, remembering Father Vaillant's maxim that if you said your prayers first, you would find plenty of time for other things afterward.

Going through the silent pueblo to Jacinto's door, the Bishop woke him and asked him to make a fire. While the Indian went to get the mules ready, Father Latour got his coffee-pot and tin cup out of his saddle-bags, and a round loaf of Mexican bread. With bread and black coffee, he could travel day after day. Jacinto was for starting without breakfast, but Father Latour made him sit down and share his loaf. Bread is never too plenty in Indian households. Clara was still lying on the settle with her baby.

At four o'clock they were on the road, Jacinto riding the mule that carried the blankets. He knew the trails through his own mountains well enough to follow them in the dark. Toward noon the Bishop suggested a halt to rest the mules, but his guide looked at the sky and shook his head. The sun was nowhere to be seen, the air was thick and grey and smelled of snow. Very soon the snow began to fall—lightly at first, but all the while becoming heavier. The vista of pine trees ahead of them grew shorter and shorter through the vast powdering of descending flakes. A little after midday a burst of wind sent the snow whirling in coils about the two travellers, and a great storm broke. The wind was like a hurricane at sea, and the air became blind with snow. The Bishop could scarcely see his guide—saw only parts of him, now a head, now a shoulder, now only the black rump of his mule. Pine trees by the way stood out for a moment, then disappeared absolutely in the whirlpool of snow. Trail and landmarks, the mountain itself, were obliterated.

Jacinto sprang from his mule and unstrapped the roll of blankets. Throwing the saddle-bags to the Bishop, he shouted, "Come, I know a place. Be quick, Padre."

The Bishop protested they could not leave the mules. Jacinto said the mules must take their chance.

For Father Latour the next hour was a test of endurance. He was blind and breathless, panting through his open mouth. He clambered over half-visible rocks, fell over prostrate trees, sank into deep holes and struggled out, always following the red blankets on the shoulders of the Indian boy, which stuck out when the boy himself was lost to sight.

Suddenly the snow seemed thinner. The guide stopped short. They were standing, the Bishop made out, under an overhanging wall of rock which made a barrier against the storm. Jacinto dropped the blankets from his shoulder and seemed to be preparing to climb the cliff. Looking up, the Bishop saw a peculiar formation in the rocks; two rounded ledges, one directly over the other, with a mouthlike opening between. They suggested two great stone lips, slightly parted and thrust outward. Up to this mouth Jacinto climbed quickly by footholds well known to him. Having mounted, he lay down on the lower lip, and helped the Bishop to clamber up. He told Father Latour to wait for him on this projection while he brought up the baggage.

A few moments later the Bishop slid after Jacinto and the blankets, through the orifice, into the throat of the cave. Within stood a wooden ladder, like that used in kivas, and down this he easily made his way to the floor.

He found himself in a lofty cavern, shaped somewhat like a Gothic chapel, of vague outline,—the only light within was that which came through the narrow aperture between the stone lips. Great as was his need of shelter, the Bishop, on his way down the ladder, was struck by a reluctance, an extreme distaste for the place. The air in the cave was glacial, penetrated to the very bones, and he detected at once a fetid odour, not very strong but highly disagreeable. Some twenty feet or so above his head the open mouth let in grey daylight like a high transom.

While he stood gazing about, trying to reckon the size of the cave, his guide was intensely preoccupied in making a careful examination of the floor and walls. At the foot of the ladder lay a heap of half-burned logs. There had been a fire there, and it had been extinguished with fresh earth,—a pile of dust covered what had been the heart of the fire. Against the cavern wall was a heap of piñon faggots, neatly piled. After he had made a minute examination of the floor, the guide began cautiously to move this pile of wood, taking the sticks up one by one, and putting them in another spot. The Bishop supposed he would make a fire at once, but he seemed in no haste to do so. Indeed, when he had moved the wood he sat down upon the floor and fell into reflection. Father Latour urged him to build a fire without further delay.

"Padre," said the Indian boy, "I do not know if it was right to bring you here. This place is used by my people for ceremonies and is known only to us. When you go out from here, you must forget."

"I will forget, certainly. But unless we can have a fire, we had better go back into the storm. I feel ill here already."

Jacinto unrolled the blankets and threw the dryest one about the shivering priest. Then he bent over the pile of ashes and charred wood, but what he did was to select a number of small stones that had been used to fence in the burning embers. These he gathered in his *sarape* and carried to the rear wall of the cavern, where, a little above his head, there seemed to be a hole. It was about as large as a very big watermelon, of an irregular oval shape.

Holes of that shape are common in the black volcanic cliffs of the Pajarito Plateau, where they occur in great numbers. This one was solitary, dark, and seemed to lead into another cavern. Though it lay higher than Jacinto's head, it was not beyond easy reach of his arms, and to the Bishop's astonishment he began deftly and noiselessly to place the stones he had collected within the mouth of this orifice, fitting them together until he had entirely closed it. He then cut wedges from the piñon faggots and inserted them into the cracks between the stones. Finally, he took a handful of the earth that had been used to smother the dead fire, and mixed it with the wet snow that had blown in between the stone lips. With this thick mud he plastered over his masonry, and smoothed it with his palm. The whole operation did not take a quarter of an hour.

Without comment or explanation he then proceeded to build a fire. The odour so disagreeable to the Bishop soon vanished before the fragrance of the burning logs. The heat seemed to purify the rank air at the same time that it took away the deathly chill, but the dizzy noise in Father Latour's head persisted. At first he thought it was a vertigo, a roaring in his ears brought on by cold and changes in his circulation. But as he grew warm and relaxed, he perceived an extraordinary vibration in this cavern; it hummed like a hive of bees, like a heavy roll of distant drums. After a time he asked Jacinto whether he, too, noticed this. The slim Indian boy smiled for the first time since they had entered the cave. He took up a faggot for a torch, and beckoned the Padre to follow him along a tunnel which ran back into the mountain, where the roof grew much lower, almost within reach of the hand. There Jacinto knelt down over a fissure in the stone floor, like a crack in china, which was plastered up with clay. Digging some of this out with his hunting knife, he put his ear on the opening, listened a few seconds, and motioned the Bishop to do likewise.

Father Latour lay with his ear to this crack for a long while, despite the cold that arose from it. He told himself he was listening to one of the oldest voices of the earth. What he heard was the sound of a great underground river, flowing through a resounding cavern. The water was far, far below, perhaps as deep as the foot of the mountain, a flood moving in utter blackness under ribs of antediluvian rock. It was not a rushing noise, but the sound of a great flood moving with majesty and power.

"It is terrible," he said at last, as he rose.

"*Si, Padre.*" Jacinto began spitting on the clay he had gouged out of the seam, and plastered it up again.

When they returned to the fire, the patch of daylight up between the two lips had grown much paler. The Bishop saw it die with regret. He took from his saddlebags his coffee-pot and a loaf of bread and a goat cheese. Jacinto climbed up to the lower ledge of the entrance, shook a pine tree, and filled the coffee-pot and one of the blankets with fresh snow. While his guide was thus engaged, the Bishop took a swallow of old Taos whisky from his pocket flask. He never liked to drink spirits in the presence of an Indian.

Jacinto declared that he thought himself lucky to get bread and black coffee. As he handed the Bishop back his tin cup after drinking its contents, he rubbed his hand over his wide sash with a smile of pleasure that showed all his white teeth.

"We had good luck to be near here," he said. "When we leave the mules, I think I can find my way here, but I am not sure. I have not been here very many times. You was scare, Padre?"

The Bishop reflected, "You hardly gave me time to be scared, boy. Were you?"

The Indian shrugged his shoulders. "I think not to return to pueblo," he admitted.

Father Latour read his breviary long by the light of the fire. Since early morning his mind had been on other than spiritual things. At last he felt that he could sleep. He made Jacinto repeat a *Pater Noster* with him, as he always did on their night camps, rolled himself in his blankets, and stretched out, feet to the fire. He had it in his mind, however, to waken in the night and study a little the curious hole his guide had so carefully closed. After he put on the mud, Jacinto had never looked in the direction of that hole again, and Father Latour, observing Indian good manners, had tried not to glance toward it.

He did waken, and the fire was still giving off a rich glow of light in that lofty Gothic chamber. But there against the wall was his guide, standing on some invisible foothold, his arms outstretched against the rock, his body flattened against it, his ear over that patch of fresh mud, listening; listening with supersensual ear, it seemed, and he looked to be supported against the rock by the intensity of his solicitude. The Bishop closed his eyes without making a sound and wondered why he had supposed he could catch his guide asleep.

The next morning they crawled out through the stone lips, and dropped into a gleaming white world. The snow-clad mountains were red in the rising sun. The Bishop stood looking down over ridge after ridge of wintry fir trees with the tender morning breaking over them, all their branches laden with soft, rose-coloured clouds of virgin snow.

Jacinto said it would not be worth while to look for the mules. When the snow melted, he would recover the saddles and bridles. They floundered on foot some eight miles to a squatter's cabin, rented horses, and completed their journey by starlight. When they reached Father Vaillant, he was sitting up in a bed of buffalo skins, his fever broken, already on the way to recovery. Another good friend had reached him before the Bishop. Kit Carson, on a deer hunt in the mountains with two Taos Indians, had heard that this village was stricken and that the Vicario was there. He hurried to the rescue, and got into the pueblo with a pack of venison meat just before the storm broke. As soon as Father Vaillant could sit in the saddle, Carson and the Bishop took him back to Santa Fé, breaking the journey into four days because of his enfeebled state.

The Bishop kept his word, and never spoke of Jacinto's cave to anyone, but he did not cease from wondering about it. It flashed into his mind from time to time, and always with a shudder of repugnance quite unjustified by anything he had experienced there. It had been a hospitable shelter to him in his extremity. Yet afterward he remembered the storm itself, even his exhaustion, with a tingling sense of pleasure. But the cave, which had probably saved his life, he remembered with horror. No tales of wonder, he told himself, would ever tempt him into a cavern hereafter.

At home again, in his own house, he still felt a certain curiosity about this ceremonial cave, and Jacinto's puzzling behaviour. It seemed almost to lend a colour of probability to some of those unpleasant stories about the Pecos religion. He was already convinced that neither the white men nor the Mexicans in Santa Fé understood anything about Indian beliefs or the workings of the Indian mind.

Kit Carson had told him that the proprietor of the trading post between Glorieta Pass and the Pecos pueblo had grown up a neighbour to these Indians, and knew as much about them as anybody. His parents had kept the trading post before him, and his mother was the first white woman in that neighborhood. The trader's name was Zeb Orchard; he lived alone in the mountains, selling salt and sugar and whisky and tobacco to red men and white. Carson said that he was honest and truthful, a good friend to the Indians, and had at one time wanted to marry a Pecos girl, but his old mother, who was very proud of being "white," would not hear of it, and so he had remained a single man and a recluse.

Father Latour made a point of stopping for the night with this trader on one of his missionary journeys, in order to question him about the Pecos customs and ceremonies.

Orchard said that the legend about the undying fire was unquestionably true; but it was kept burning, not in the mountain, but in their own pueblo. It was a smothered fire in a clay oven, and had been burning in one of the kivas ever since the pueblo was founded, centuries ago. About the snake stories, he was not certain. He had seen rattlesnakes around the pueblo, to be sure, but there were rattlers everywhere. A Pecos boy had been bitten on the ankle some years ago, and had come to him for whisky, he swelled up and was very sick, like any other boy.

The Bishop asked Orchard if he thought it probable that the Indians kept a great serpent in concealment somewhere, as was commonly reported.

"They do keep some sort of varmint out in the mountain, that they bring in for their religious ceremonies," the trader said. "But I don't know if it's a snake or not. No white man knows anything about Indian religion, Padre."

As they talked further, Orchard admitted that when he was a boy he had been very curious about these snake stories himself, and once, at their festival time, he had spied on the Pecos men, though that was not a very safe thing to do. He had lain in ambush for two nights on the mountain, and he saw a party of Indians bringing in a chest by torch-light. It was about the size of a woman's trunk, and it was heavy enough to bend the young aspen poles on which it was hung. "If I'd seen white men bringing in a chest after dark," he observed, "I could have made a guess at what was in it; money, or whisky, or fire-arms. But seeing it was Indians, I can't say. It might have been only queer-shaped rocks their ancestors had taken a notion to. The things they value most are worth nothing to us. They've got their own superstitions, and their minds will go round and round in the same old ruts till Judgment Day."

Father Latour remarked that their veneration for old customs was a quality he liked in the Indians, and that it played a great part in his own religion.

The trader told him he might make good Catholics among the Indians, but he would never separate them from their own beliefs. "Their priests have their own kind of mysteries. I don't know how much of it is real and how much is made up. I remember something that happened when I was a little fellow. One night a Pecos girl, with her baby in her arms, ran into the kitchen here and begged my mother to hide her until after the festival, for she'd seen signs between the *caciques*, and was sure they were going to feed her baby to the snake. Whether it was true or not, she certainly believed it, poor thing, and Mother let her stay. It made a great impression on me at the time."

DEATH COMES FOR THE ARCHBISHOP

BOOK FIVE

Padre Martínez

1
The Old Order

Bishop Latour, with Jacinto, was riding through the mountains on his first official visit to Taos—after Albuquerque, the largest and richest parish in his diocese. Both the priest and people there were hostile to Americans and jealous of interference. Any European, except a Spaniard, was regarded as a gringo. The Bishop had let the parish alone, giving their animosity plenty of time to cool. With Carson's help he had informed himself fully about conditions there, and about the powerful old priest, Antonio José Martínez, who was ruler in temporal as well as in spiritual affairs. Indeed, before Father Latour's entrance upon the scene, Martínez had been dictator to all the parishes in northern New Mexico, and the native priests at Santa Fé were all of them under his thumb.

It was common talk that Padre Martínez had instigated the revolt of the Taos Indians five years ago, when Bent, the American Governor, and a dozen other white men were murdered and scalped. Seven of the Taos Indians had been tried before a military court and hanged for the murder, but no attempt had been made to call the plotting priest to account. Indeed, Padre Martínez had managed to profit considerably by the affair.

The Indians who were sentenced to death had sent for their Padre and begged him to get them out of the trouble he had got them into. Martínez promised to save their lives if they would deed him their lands, near the pueblo. This they did, and after the conveyance was properly executed the Padre troubled himself no more about the matter, but went to pay a visit at his native town of Abiquiu. In his absence the seven Indians were hanged on the appointed day. Martínez now cultivated their fertile farms, which made him quite the richest man in the parish.

Father Latour had had polite correspondence with Martínez, but had met him only once, on that memorable occasion when the Padre had ridden up from Taos to strengthen the Santa Fé clergy in their refusal to recognize the new Bishop. But he could see him as if that were only yesterday,—the priest of Taos was not a man one would easily forget. One could not have passed him on the street without feeling his great physical force and his imperious will. Not much taller than the Bishop in reality, he gave the impression of being an enormous man. His broad high shoulders were like a bull buffalo's, his big head was set defiantly on a thick neck, and the full-cheeked, richly coloured, egg-shaped Spanish face—how vividly the Bishop remembered that face! It was so unusual that he would be glad to see it again; a high, narrow forehead, brilliant yellow eyes set deep in strong arches, and full, florid cheeks,—not blank areas of smooth flesh, as in Anglo-Saxon faces, but full of muscular activity, as quick to change with feeling as any of his features. His mouth was the very assertion of violent, uncurbed passions and tyrannical self-will; the full lips thrust out and taut, like the flesh of animals distended by fear or desire.

Father Latour judged that the day of lawless personal power was almost over, even on the frontier, and this figure was to him already like something picturesque and impressive, but really impotent, left over from the past.

The Bishop and Jacinto left the mountains behind them, the trail dropped to a plain covered by clumps of very old sage-brush, with trunks as thick as a man's leg. Jacinto pointed out a cloud of dust moving rapidly toward them,—a cavalcade of a hundred men or more, Indians and Mexicans, come out to welcome their Bishop with shouting and musketry.

As the horsemen approached, Padre Martínez himself was easily distinguishable—in buckskin breeches, high boots and silver spurs, a wide Mexican hat on his head, and a great black cape wound about his shoulders like a shepherd's plaid. He rode up to the Bishop and reining in his black gelding, uncovered his head in a broad salutation, while his escort surrounded the churchmen and fired their muskets into the air.

The two priests rode side by side into Los Ranchos de Taos, a little town of yellow walls and winding streets and green orchards. The inhabitants were all gathered in the square before the church. When the Bishop dismounted to enter the church, the women threw their shawls on the dusty pathway for him to walk upon, and as he passed through the kneeling congregation, men and women snatched for his hand to kiss the Episcopal ring. In his own country all this would have been highly distasteful to Jean Marie Latour. Here, these demonstrations seemed a part of the high colour that was in landscape and gardens, in the flaming cactus and the gaudily decorated altars,—in the agonized Christs and dolorous Virgins and the very human figures of the saints. He had already learned that with this people religion was necessarily theatrical.

From Los Ranchos the party rode quickly across the grey plain into Taos itself, to the priest's house, opposite the church, where a great throng had collected. As the people sank on their knees, one boy, a gawky lad of ten or twelve, remained standing, his mouth open and his hat on his head. Padre Martínez reached over the heads of several kneeling women, snatched off the boy's cap, and cuffed him soundly about the ears. When Father Latour murmured in protest, the native priest said boldly:

"He is my own son, Bishop, and it is time I taught him manners."

So this was to be the tune, the Bishop reflected. His well-schooled countenance did not change a shadow as he received this challenge, and he passed on into the Padre's house. They went at once into Martínez's study, where they found a young man lying on the floor, fast asleep. He was a very large young man, very stout, lying on his back with his head pillowed on a book, and as he breathed his bulk rose and fell amazingly. He wore a Franciscan's brown gown, and his hair was clipped short. At sight of the sleeper, Padre Martínez broke into a laugh and gave him a not very gentle kick in the ribs. The fellow got to his feet in great confusion, escaping through a door into the *patio*.

"You there," the Padre called after him, "only young men who work hard at night want to sleep in the day! You must have been studying by candle-light. I'll give you an examination in theology!" This was greeted by a titter of feminine laughter from the windows across the court, where the fugitive took refuge behind a washing hung out to dry. He bent his tall, full figure and disappeared between a pair of wet sheets.

"That was my student, Trinidad," said Martínez, "a nephew of my old friend Father Lucero, at Arroyo Hondo. He's a monk, but we want him to take orders. We sent him to the Seminary in Durango, but he was either too homesick or too stupid to learn anything, so I'm teaching him here. We shall make a priest of him one day."

Father Latour was told to consider the house his own, but he had no wish to. The disorder was almost more than his fastidious taste could bear. The Padre's study table was sprinkled with snuff, and piled so high with books that they almost hid the crucifix hanging behind it. Books were heaped on chairs and tables all over the house,—and the books and the floors were deep in the dust of spring sand-storms. Father Martínez's boots and hats lay about in corners, his coats and cassocks were hung on pegs and draped over pieces of furniture. Yet the place seemed over-run by serving-women, young and old,—and by large yellow cats with full soft fur, of a special breed, apparently. They slept in the window-sills, lay on the well-curb in the *patio;* the boldest came, directly, to the supper-table, where their master fed them carelessly from his plate.

When they sat down to supper, the host introduced to the Bishop the tall, stout young man with the protruding front, who had been asleep on the floor. He said again that Trinidad Lucero was studying with him, and was supposed to be his secretary,—adding that he spent most of his time hanging about the kitchen and hindering the girls at their work.

These remarks were made in the young man's presence, but did not embarrass him at all. His whole attention was fixed upon the mutton stew, which he began to devour with undue haste as soon as his plate was put before him. The Bishop observed later that Trinidad was treated very much like a poor relation or a servant. He was sent on errands, was told without ceremony to fetch the Padre's boots, to bring wood for the fire, to saddle his horse. Father Latour disliked his personality so much that he could scarcely look at him. His fat face was irritatingly stupid, and had the grey, oily look of soft cheeses. The corners of his mouth were deep folds in plumpness, like the creases in a baby's legs, and the steel rim of his spectacles, where it crossed his nose, was embedded in soft flesh. He said not one word during supper, but ate as if he were afraid of never seeing food again. When his attention left his plate for a moment, it was fixed in the same greedy way upon the girl who served the table—and who seemed to regard him with careless contempt. The student gave the impression of being always stupefied by one form of sensual disturbance or another.

Padre Martínez, with a napkin tied round his neck to protect his cassock, ate and drank generously. The Bishop found the food poor enough, despite the many cooks, though the wine, which came from El Paso del Norte, was very fair.

During supper, his host asked the Bishop flatly if he considered celibacy an essential condition of the priest's vocation.

Father Latour replied merely that this question had been thrashed out many centuries ago and decided once for all.

"Nothing is decided once for all," Martínez declared fiercely. "Celibacy may be all very well for the French clergy, but not for ours. St. Augustine himself says it is better not to go against nature. I find every evidence that in his old age he regretted having practised continence."

The Bishop said he would be interested to see the passages from which he drew such conclusions, observing that he knew the writings of St. Augustine fairly well.

"I have the telling passages all written down somewhere. I will find them before you go. You have probably read them with a sealed mind. Celibate priests lose their perceptions. No priest can experience repentance and forgiveness of sin unless he himself falls into sin. Since concupiscence is the most common form of temptation, it is better for him to know something about it. The soul cannot be humbled by fasts and prayer; it must be broken by mortal sin to experience forgiveness of sin and rise to a state of grace. Otherwise, religion is nothing but dead logic."

"This is a subject upon which we must confer later, and at some length," said the Bishop quietly. "I shall reform these practices throughout my diocese as rapidly as possible. I hope it will be but a short time until there is not a priest left who does not keep all the vows he took when he bound himself to the service of the altar."

The swarthy Padre laughed, and threw off the big cat which had mounted to his shoulder. "It will keep you busy, Bishop. Nature has got the start of you here. But for all that, our native priests are more devout than your French Jesuits. We have a living Church here, not a dead arm of the European Church. Our religion grew out of the soil, and has its own roots. We pay a filial respect to the person of the holy Father, but Rome has no authority here. We do not require aid from the Propaganda, and we resent its interference. The Church the Franciscan Fathers planted here was cut off; this the second growth, and is indigenous. Our people are the most devout left in the world. If you blast their faith by European formalities, they will become infidels and profligates."

To this eloquence the Bishop returned blandly that he had not come to deprive the people of their religion, but that he would be compelled to deprive some of the priests of their parishes if they did not change their way of life.

Father Martínez filled his glass and replied with perfect good humour. "You cannot deprive me of mine, Bishop. Try it! I will organize my own church. You can have your French priest of Taos, and I will have the people!"

With this the Padre left the table and stood warming his back at the fire, his cassock pulled up about his waist to expose his trousers to the blaze. "You are a young man, my Bishop," he went on, rolling his big head back and looking up at the well-smoked roof poles. "And you know nothing about Indians or Mexicans. If you try to introduce European civilization here and change our old ways, to interfere with the secret dances of the Indians, let us say, or abolish the bloody rites of the Penitentes, I foretell an early death for you. I advise you to study our native traditions before you begin your reforms. You are among barbarous people, my Frenchman, between two savage races. The dark things forbidden by your Church are a part of Indian religion. You cannot introduce French fashions here."

At this moment the student, Trinidad, got up quietly, and after an obsequious bow to the Bishop, went with soft, escaping tread toward the kitchen. When his brown skirt had disappeared through the door, Father Latour turned sharply to his host.

"Martínez, I consider it very unseemly to talk in this loose fashion before young men, especially a young man who is studying for the priesthood. Furthermore, I cannot see why a young man of this calibre should be encouraged to take orders. He will never hold a parish in my diocese."

Padre Martínez laughed and showed his long, yellow teeth. Laughing did not become him; his teeth were too large—distinctly vulgar. "Oh, Trinidad will go to Arroyo Hondo as curate to his uncle, who is growing old. He's a very devout fellow, Trinidad. You ought to see him in Passion Week. He goes up to Abiquiu and becomes another man; carries the heaviest crosses to the highest mountains, and takes more scourging than anyone. He comes back here with his back so full of cactus spines that the girls have to pick him like a chicken."

Father Latour was tired, and went to his room soon after supper. The bed, upon examination, seemed clean and comfortable, but he felt uncertain of its surroundings. He did not like the air of this house. After he retired, the clatter of dish-washing and the giggling of women across the *patio* kept him awake a long while; and when that ceased, Father Martínez began snoring in some chamber near by. He must have left his door open into the *patio,* for the adobe partitions were thick enough to smother sound otherwise. The Padre snored like an enraged bull, until the Bishop decided to go forth and find his door and close it. He arose, lit his candle, and opened his own door in half-hearted resolution. As the night wind blew into the room, a little dark shadow fluttered from the wall across the floor; a mouse, perhaps. But no, it was a bunch of woman's hair that had been indolently tossed into a corner when some slovenly female toilet was made in this room. This discovery annoyed the Bishop exceedingly.

High Mass was at eleven the next morning, the parish priest officiating and the Bishop in the Episcopal chair. He was well pleased with the church of Taos. The building was clean and in good repair, the congregation large and devout. The delicate lace, snowy linen, and burnished brass on the altar told of a devoted Altar Guild. The boys who served at the altar wore rich smocks of hand-made lace over their scarlet cassocks. The Bishop had never heard the Mass more impressively sung than by Father Martínez. The man had a beautiful baritone voice, and he drew from some deep well of emotional power. Nothing in the service was slighted, every phrase and gesture had its full value. At the moment of the Elevation the dark priest seemed to give his whole force, his swarthy body and all its blood, to that lifting-up. Rightly guided, the Bishop reflected, this Mexican might have been a great man. He had an altogether compelling personality, a disturbing, mysterious, magnetic power.

After the confirmation service, Father Martínez had horses brought round and took the Bishop out to see his farms and live-stock. He took him all over his ranches down in the rich bottom lands between Taos and the Indian pueblo which, as Father Latour knew, had come into his possession from the seven Indians who were hanged. Martínez referred carelessly to the Bent massacre as they rode along. He boasted that there had never been trouble afoot in New Mexico that wasn't started in Taos.

They stopped just west of the pueblo a little before sunset,—a pueblo very different from all the others the Bishop had visited; two large communal houses, shaped like pyramids, gold-coloured in the afternoon light, with the purple mountain lying just behind them. Gold-coloured men in white burnouses came out on the stairlike flights of roofs, and stood still as statues, apparently watching the changing light on the mountain. There was a religious silence over the place; no sound at all but the bleating of goats coming home through clouds of golden dust.

These two houses, the Padre told him, had been continuously occupied by this tribe for more than a thousand years. Coronado's men found them there, and described them as a superior kind of Indian, handsome and dignified in bearing, dressed in deerskin coats and trousers like those of Europeans.

Though the mountain was timbered, its lines were so sharp that it had the sculptured look of naked mountains like the Sandias. The general growth on its sides was evergreen, but the canyons and ravines were wooded with aspens, so that the shape of every depression was painted on the mountain-side, light green against the dark, like symbols; serpentine, crescent, half-circles. This mountain and its ravines had been the seat of old religious ceremonies, honeycombed with noiseless Indian life, the repository of Indian secrets, for many centuries, the Padre remarked.

"And some place in there, you may be sure, they keep Popé's estufa, but no white man will ever see it. I mean the estufa where Popé sealed himself up for four years and never saw the light of day, when he was planning the revolt of 1680. I suppose you know all about that outbreak, Bishop Latour?"

"Something, of course, from the Martyrology. But I did not know that it originated in Taos."

"Haven't I just told you that all the trouble there ever was in New Mexico originated in Taos?" boasted the Padre. "Popé was born a San Juan Indian, but so was Napoleon a Corsican. He operated from Taos."

Padre Martínez knew his country, a country which had no written histories. He gave the Bishop much the best account he had heard of the great Indian revolt of 1680, which added such a long chapter to the Martyrology of the New World, when all the Spaniards were killed or driven out, and there was not one European left alive north of El Paso del Norte.

That night after supper, as his host sat taking snuff, Father Latour questioned him closely and learned something about the story of his life.

Martínez was born directly under that solitary blue mountain on the sky-line west of Taos, shaped like a pyramid with the apex sliced off, in Abiquiu. It was one of the oldest Mexican settlements in the territory, surrounded by canyons so deep and ranges so rugged that it was practically cut off from intercourse with the outside world. Being so solitary, its people were sombre in temperament, fierce and fanatical in religion, and celebrated the Passion Week by cross-bearings and bloody scourgings.

Antonio José Martínez grew up there, without learning to read or write, married at twenty, and lost his wife and child when he was twenty-three. After his marriage he had learned to read from the parish priest, and when he became a widower he decided to study for the priesthood. Taking his clothes and the little money he got from the sale of his household goods, he started on horseback for Durango, in Old Mexico. There he entered the Seminary and began a life of laborious study.

The Bishop could imagine what it meant for a young man who had not learned to read until long after adolescence, to undergo a severe academic training. He found Martínez deeply versed, not only in the Church Fathers, but in the Latin and Spanish classics. After six years at the Seminary, Martínez had returned to his native Abiquiu as priest of the parish church there. He was passionately attached to that old village under the pyramidal mountain. All the while he had been in Taos, half a lifetime now, he made periodic pilgrimages on horseback back to Abiquiu, as if the flavour of his own yellow earth were medicine to his soul. Naturally he hated the Americans. The American occupation meant the end of men like himself. He was a man of the old order, a son of Abiquiu, and his day was over.

On his departure from Taos, the Bishop went out of his way to make a call at Kit Carson's ranch house. Carson, he knew, was away buying sheep, but Father Latour wished to see the Señora Carson to thank her again for her kindness to poor Magdalena, and to tell her of the woman's happy and devoted life with the Sisters in the school at Santa Fé.

The Señora received him with that quiet but unabashed hospitality which is a common grace in Mexican households. She was a tall woman, slender, with drooping shoulders and lustrous black eyes and hair. Though she could not read, both her face and conversation were intelligent. To the Bishop's thinking, she was handsome; her countenance showed that discipline of life which he admired. She had a cheerful disposition, too, and a pleasant sense of humour. It was possible to talk confidentially to her. She said she hoped he had been comfortable in Padre Martínez's house, with an inflection which told that she much doubted it, and she laughed a little when he confessed that he had been annoyed by the presence of Trinidad Lucero.

"Some people say he is Father Lucero's son," she said with a shrug. "But I do not think so. More likely one of Padre Martínez's. Did you hear what happened to him at Abiquiu last year, in Passion Week? He tried to be like the Saviour, and had himself crucified. Oh, not with nails! He was tied upon a cross with ropes, to hang there all night; they do that sometimes at Abiquiu, it is a very old-fashioned place. But he is so heavy that after he had hung there a few hours, the cross fell over with him, and he was very much humiliated. Then he had himself tied to a post and said he would bear as many stripes as our Saviour—six thousand, as was revealed to St. Bridget. But before they had given him a hundred, he fainted. They scourged him with cactus whips, and his back was so poisoned that he was sick up there for a long while. This year they sent word that they did not want him at Abiquiu, so he had to keep Holy Week here, and everybody laughed at him."

Father Latour asked the Señora to tell him frankly whether she thought he could put a stop to the extravagances of the Penitential Brotherhood. She smiled and shook her head. "I often say to my husband, I hope you will not try to do that. It would only set the people against you. The old people have need of their old customs; and the young ones will go with the times."

As the Bishop was taking his leave, she put into his saddle-bags a beautiful piece of lace-work for Magdalena. "She will not be likely to use it for herself, but she will be glad to have it to give to the Sisters. That brutal man left her nothing. After he was hung, there was nothing to sell but his gun and one burro. That was why he was going to take the risk of killing two Padres for their mules—and for spite against religion, maybe! Magdelena said he had often threatened to kill the priest at Mora."

At Santa Fé the Bishop found Father Vaillant awaiting him. They had not seen each other since Easter, and there were many things to be discussed. The vigour and zeal of Bishop Latour's administration had already been recognized at Rome, and he had lately received a letter from Cardinal Fransoni, Prefect of the Propaganda, announcing that the vicarate of Santa Fé had been formally raised to a diocese. By the same long-delayed post came an invitation from the Cardinal, urgently requesting Father Latour's presence at important conferences at the Vatican during the following year. Though all these matters must be taken up in their turn between the Bishop and his Vicar-General, Father Joseph had undoubtedly come up from Albuquerque at this particular time because of a lively curiosity to hear how the Bishop had been received in Taos.

Seated in the study in their old cassocks, with the candles lighted on the table between them, they spent a long evening.

"For the present," Father Latour remarked, "I shall do nothing to change the curious situation at Taos. It is not expedient to interfere. The church is strong, the people are devout. No matter what the conduct of the priest has been, he has built up a strong organization, and his people are devotedly loyal to him."

"But can he be disciplined, do you think?"

"Oh, there is no question of discipline! He has been a little potentate too long. His people would assuredly support him against a French Bishop. For the present I shall be blind to what I do not like there."

"But Jean," Father Joseph broke out in agitation, "the man's life is an open scandal, one hears of it everywhere. Only a few weeks ago I was told a pitiful story of a Mexican girl carried off in one of the Indian raids on the Costella valley. She was a child of eight when she was carried away, and was fifteen when she was found and ransomed. During all that time the pious girl had preserved her virginity by a succession of miracles. She had a medal from the shrine of Our Lady of Guadalupe tied round her neck, and she said such prayers as she had been taught. Her chastity was threatened many times, but always some unexpected event averted the catastrophe. After she was found and sent back to some relatives living in Arroyo Hondo, she was so devout that she wished to become a religious. She was debauched by this Martínez, and he married her to one of his peons. She is now living on one of his farms."

"Yes, Christóbal told me that story," said the Bishop with a shrug. "But Padre Martínez is getting too old to play the part of Don Juan much longer. I do not wish to lose the parish of Taos in order to punish its priest, my friend. I have no priest strong enough to put in his place. You are the only man who could meet the situation there, and you are at Albuquerque. A year from now I shall be in Rome, and there I hope to get a Spanish missionary who will take over the parish of Taos. Only a Spaniard would be welcomed there, I think."

"You are doubtless right," said Father Joseph. "I am often too hasty in my judgments. I may do very badly for you while you are in Europe. For I suppose I am to leave my dear Albuquerque, and come to Santa Fé while you are gone?"

"Assuredly. They will love you all the more for lacking you awhile. I hope to bring some more hardy Auvergnats back with me, young men from our own Seminary, and I am afraid I must put one of them in Albuquerque. You have been there long enough. You have done all that is necessary. I need you here, Father Joseph. As it is now, one of us must ride seventy miles whenever we wish to converse about anything."

Father Vaillant sighed. "Ah, I supposed it would come! You will snatch me from Albuquerque as you did from Sandusky. When I went there everybody was my enemy, now everybody is my friend; therefore it is time to go." Father Vaillant took off his glasses, folded them, and put them in their case, which act always announced his determination to retire. "So a year from now you will be in Rome. Well, I had rather be among my people in Albuquerque, that I can say honestly. But Clermont—there I envy you. I should like to see my own mountains again. At least you will see all my family and bring me word of them, and you can bring me the vestments that my dear Sister Philomène and her nuns have been making for me these three years. I shall be very glad to have them." He rose, and took up one of the candles. "And when you leave Clermont, Jean, put a few chestnuts in your pocket for me!"

2
The Miser

In February Bishop Latour once more set out on horseback over the Santa Fé trail, this time with Rome as his objective. He was absent for nearly a year, and when he returned he brought with him four young priests from his own Seminary of Montferrand, and a Spanish priest, Father Taladrid, whom he had found in Rome, and who was at once sent to Taos. At the Bishop's suggestion, Padre Martínez formally resigned his parish, with the understanding that he was still to celebrate Mass upon solemn occasions. Not only did he avail himself of this privilege, but he continued to perform all marriages and burial services and to dictate the lives of the parishioners. Very soon he and Father Taladrid were at open war.

When the Bishop, unable to compose their differences, supported the new priest, Father Martínez and his friend Father Lucero, of Arroyo Hondo, mutinied; flatly refused to submit, and organized a church of their own. This, they declared, was the old Holy Catholic Church of Mexico, while the Bishop's church was an American institution. In both towns the greater part of the population went over to the schismatic church, though some pious Mexicans, in great perplexity, attended Mass at both. Father Martínez printed a long and eloquent Proclamation (which very few of his parishioners could read) giving an historical justification for his schism, and denying the obligation of celibacy for the priesthood. As both he and Father Lucero were well on in years, this particular clause could be of little benefit to anyone in their new organization except Trinidad. After the two old priests went off into schism, one of their first solemn acts was to elevate Father Lucero's nephew to the priesthood, and he acted as curate to them both, swinging back and forth between Taos and Arroyo Hondo.

The schismatic church at least accomplished the rejuvenation of the two rebellious priests at its head, and far and wide revived men's interest in them,—though they had always furnished their people with plenty to talk about. Ever since they were young men with adjoining parishes, they had been friends, cronies, rivals, sometimes bitter enemies. But their quarrels could never keep them apart for long.

Old Marino Lucero had not one trait in common with Martínez, except the love of authority. He had been a miser from his youth, and lived down in the sunken world of Arroyo Hondo in the barest poverty, though he was supposed to be very rich. He used to boast that his house was as poor as a burro's stable. His bed, his crucifix, and his bean-pot were his furniture. He kept no live-stock but one poor mule, on which he rode over to Taos to quarrel with his friend Martínez, or to get a solid dinner when he was hungry. In his *casa* every day was Friday—unless one of his neighbour women cooked a chicken and brought it in to him out of pure compassion. For his people liked him. He was grasping, but not oppressive, and he wrung more pesos out of Arroyo Seco and Questa than out of his own arroyo. Thrift is such a rare quality among Mexicans that they find it very amusing; his people loved to tell how he never bought anything, but picked up old brooms after housewives had thrown them away, and that he wore Padre Martínez's garments after the Padre would have them no longer, though they were so much too big for him. One of the priests' fiercest quarrels had come about because Martínez gave some of his old clothes to a monk from Mexico who was studying at his house, and who had not wherewithal to cover himself as winter came on.

The two priests had always talked shamelessly about each other. All Martínez's best stories were about Lucero, and all Lucero's were about Martínez.

"You see how it is," Padre Lucero would say to the young men at a wedding party, "my way is better than old José Martínez's. His nose and chin are getting to be close neighbours now, and a petticoat is not much good to him any more. But I can still rise upright at the sight of a dollar. With a new piece of money in my hand I am happier than ever; and what can he do with a pretty girl but regret?"

Avarice, he assured them, was the one passion that grew stronger and sweeter in old age. He had the lust for money as Martínez had for women, and they had never been rivals in the pursuit of their pleasures. After Trinidad was ordained and went to stay with his uncle, Father Lucero complained that he had formed gross habits living with Martínez, and was eating him out of house and home. Father Martínez told with delight how Trinidad sponged upon the parish at Arroyo Hondo, and went about poking his nose into one bean-pot after another.

When the Bishop could no longer remain deaf to the rebellion, he sent Father Vaillant over to Taos to publish the warning for three weeks and exhort the two priests to renounce their heresy. On the fourth Sunday Father Joseph, who complained that he was always sent *"à fouetter les chats,"* solemnly read the letter in which the Bishop stripped Father Martínez of the rights and privileges of the priesthood. On the afternoon of the same day, he rode over to Arroyo Hondo, eighteen miles away, and read a similar letter of excommunication against Father Lucero.

Father Martínez continued at the head of his schismatic church until, after a short illness, he died and was buried in schism, by Father Lucero. Soon after this, Father Lucero himself fell into a decline. But even after he was ailing he performed a feat which became one of the legends of the countryside,—killed a robber in a midnight scuffle.

A wandering teamster who had been discharged from a wagon train for theft, was picking up a living over in Taos and there heard the stories about Father Lucero's hidden riches. He came to Arroyo Hondo to rob the old man. Father Lucero was a light sleeper, and hearing stealthy sounds in the middle of the night, he reached for the carving-knife he kept hidden under his mattress and sprang upon the intruder. They began fighting in the dark, and though the thief was a young man and armed, the old priest stabbed him to death and then, covered with blood, ran out to arouse the town. The neighbours found the Padre's chamber like a slaughterhouse, his victim lying dead beside the hole he had dug. They were amazed at what the old man had been able to do.

But from the shock of that night Father Lucero never recovered. He wasted away so rapidly that his people had the horse doctor come from Taos to look at him. This veterinary was a Yankee who had been successful in treating men as well as horses, but he said he could do nothing for Father Lucero; he believed he had an internal tumour or a cancer.

Padre Lucero died repentant, and Father Vaillant, who had pronounced his excommunication, was the one to reconcile him to the Church. The Vicar was in Taos on business for the Bishop, staying with Kit Carson and the Señora. They were all sitting at supper one evening during a heavy rainstorm, when a horseman rode up to the *portale*. Carson went out to receive him. The visitor he brought in with him was Trinidad Lucero, who took off his rubber coat and stood in a full-skirted cassock of Arroyo Hondo make, a crucifix about his neck, seeming to fill the room with his size and importance. After bowing ceremoniously to the Señora, he addressed himself to Father Vaillant in his best English, speaking slowly in his thick felty voice.

"I am the only nephew of Padre Lucero. My uncle is verra seek and soon to die. She has vomit the blood." He dropped his eyes.

"Speak to me in your own language, man!" cried Father Joseph. "I can at least do more with Spanish than you can with English. Now tell me what you have to say of your uncle's condition."

Trinidad gave some account of his uncle's illness, repeating solemnly the phrase, "She has vomit the blood," which he seemed to find impressive. The sick man wished to see Father Vaillant, and begged that he would come to him and give him the Sacrament.

Carson urged the Vicar to wait until morning, as the road down into "the Hondo" would be badly washed by rain and dangerous to go over in the dark. But Father Vaillant said if the road were bad he could go down on foot. Excusing himself to the Señora Carson, he went to his room to put on his riding-clothes and get his saddle-bags. Trinidad, upon invitation, sat down at the empty place and made the most of his opportunity. The host saddled Father Vaillant's mule, and the Vicar rode away, with Trinidad for guide.

Not that he needed a guide to Arroyo Hondo, it was a place especially dear to him, and he was always glad to find a pretext for going there. How often he had ridden over there on fine days in summer, or in early spring, before the green was out, when the whole country was pink and blue and yellow, like a coloured map.

One approached over a sage-brush plain that appeared to run level and unbroken to the base of the distant mountains; then without warning, one suddenly found oneself upon the brink of a precipice, of a chasm in the earth over two hundred feet deep, the sides sheer cliffs, but cliffs of earth, not rock. Drawing rein at the edge, one looked down into a sunken world of green fields and gardens, with a pink adobe town, at the bottom of this great ditch. The men and mules walking about down there, or plowing the fields, looked like the figures of a child's Noah's ark. Down the middle of the arroyo, through the sunken fields and pastures, flowed a rushing stream which came from the high mountains. Its original source was so high, indeed, that by merely laying a closed wooden trough up the face of the cliff, the Mexicans conveyed the water some hundreds of feet to an open ditch at the top of the precipice. Father Vaillant had often stopped to watch the imprisoned water leaping out into the light like a thing alive, just where the steep trail down into the Hondo began. The water thus diverted was but a tiny thread of the full creek; the main stream ran down the arroyo over a white rock bottom, with green willows and deep hay grass and brilliant wild flowers on its banks. Evening primroses, the fireweed, and butterfly weed grew to a tropical size and brilliance there among the sedges.

But this was the first time Father Vaillant had ever gone down into the Hondo after dark, and at the edge of the cliff he decided not to put Contento to so cruel a test. "He can do it," he said to Trinidad, "but I will not make him." He dismounted and went on foot down the steep winding trail.

They reached Father Lucero's house before midnight. Half the population of the town seemed to be in attendance, and the place was lit up as if for a festival. The sick man's chamber was full of Mexican women, sitting about on the floor, wrapped in their black shawls, saying their prayers with lighted candles before them. One could scarcely step for the candles.

Father Vaillant beckoned to a woman he knew well, Conçeptión Gonzales, and asked her what was the meaning of this. She whispered that the dying Padre would have it so. His sight was growing dim, and he kept calling for more lights. All his life, Conçeptión sighed, he had been so saving of candles, and had mostly done with a pine splinter in the evenings.

In the corner, on the bed, Father Lucero was groaning and tossing, one man rubbing his feet, and another wringing cloths out of hot water and putting them on his stomach to dull the pain. Señora Gonzales whispered that the sick man had been gnawing the sheets for pain; she had brought over her best ones, and they were chewed to lacework across the top.

Father Vaillant approached the bed-side, "Get away from the bed a little, my good women. Arrange yourselves along the wall, your candles blind me."

But as they began rising and lifting their candlesticks from the floor, the sick man called, "No, no, do not take away the lights! Some thief will come, and I will have nothing left."

The women shrugged, looked reproachfully at Father Vaillant, and sat down again.

Padre Lucero was wasted to the bones. His cheeks were sunken, his hooked nose was clay-coloured and waxy, his eyes were wild with fever. They burned up at Father Joseph,—great, black, glittering, distrustful eyes. On this night of his departure the old man looked more Spaniard than Mexican. He clutched Father Joseph's hand with a grip surprisingly strong, and gave the man who was rubbing his feet a vigorous kick in the chest.

"Have done with my feet there, and take away these wet rags. Now that the Vicar has come, I have something to say, and I want you all to hear." Father Lucero's voice had always been thin and high in pitch, his parishioners used to say it was like a horse talking. "Señor Vicario, you remember Padre Martínez? You ought to, for you served him as badly as you did me. Now listen:"

Father Lucero related that Martínez, before his death, had entrusted to him a certain sum of money to be spent in masses for the repose of his soul, these to be offered at his native church in Abiquiu. Lucero had not used the money as he promised, but had buried it under the dirt floor of this room, just below the large crucifix that hung on the wall yonder.

At this point Father Vaillant again signalled to the women to withdraw, but as they took up their candles, Father Lucero sat up in his night-shirt and cried, "Stay as you are! Are you going to run away and leave me with a stranger? I trust him no more than I do you! Oh, why did God not make some way for a man to protect his own after death? Alive, I can do it with my knife, old as I am. But after—?"

The Señora Gonzales soothed Father Lucero, persuaded him to lie back upon his pillows and tell them what he wanted them to do. He explained that this money which he had taken in trust from Martínez was to be sent to Abiquiu and used as the Padre had wished. Under the crucifix, and under the floor beneath the bed on which he was lying, they would find his own savings. One third of his hoard was for Trinidad. The rest was to be spent in masses for his soul, and they were to be celebrated in the old church of San Miguel in Santa Fé.

Father Vaillant assured him that all his wishes should be scrupulously carried out, and now it was time for him to dismiss the cares of this world and prepare his mind to receive the Sacrament.

"All in good time. But a man does not let go of this world so easily. Where is Conçeptión Gonzales? Come here, my daughter. See to it that the money is taken up from under the floor while I am still in this chamber, before my body is cold, that it is counted in the presence of all these women, and the sum set down in writing." At this point, the old man started, as with a new hope. "And Christóbal, he is the man! Christóbal Carson must be here to count it and set it down. He is a just man. Trinidad, you fool, why did you not bring Christóbal?"

Father Vaillant was scandalized. "Unless you compose yourself, Father Lucero, and fix your thoughts upon Heaven, I shall refuse to administer the Sacrament. In your present state of mind, it would be a sacrilege."

The old man folded his hands and closed his eyes in assent. Father Vaillant went into the adjoining room to put on his cassock and stole, and in his absence Conçeptión Gonzales covered a small table by the bed with one of her own white napkins and placed upon it two wax candles, and a cup of water for the ministrant's hands. Father Vaillant came back in his vestments, with his pyx and basin of holy water, and began sprinkling the bed and the watchers, repeating the antiphon, *Asperges me, Domine, hyssopo, et mundabor.* The women stole away, leaving their lights upon the floor. Father Lucero made his confession, renouncing his heresy and expressing contrition, after which he received the Sacrament.

The ceremony calmed the tormented man, and he lay quiet with his hands folded on his breast. The women returned and sat murmuring prayers as before. The rain drove against the window panes, the wind made a hollow sound as it sucked down through the deep arroyo. Some of the watchers were drooping from weariness, but not one showed any wish to go home. Watching beside a death-bed was not a hardship for them, but a privilege,—in the case of a dying priest it was a distinction.

In those days, even in European countries, death had a solemn social importance. It was not regarded as a moment when certain bodily organs ceased to function, but as a dramatic climax, a moment when the soul made its entrance into the next world, passing in full consciousness through a lowly door to an unimaginable scene. Among the watchers there was always the hope that the dying man might reveal something of what he alone could see; that his countenance, if not his lips, would speak, and on his features would fall some light or shadow from beyond. The "Last Words" of great men, Napoleon, Lord Byron, were still printed in gift-books, and the dying murmurs of every common man and woman were listened for and treasured by their neighbours and kins-folk. These sayings, no matter how unimportant, were given oracular significance and pondered by those who must one day go the same road.

The stillness of the death chamber was suddenly broken when Trinidad Lucero knelt down before the crucifix on the wall to pray. His uncle, though all thought him asleep, began to struggle and cry out, "A thief! Help, help!" Trinidad retired quickly, but after that the old man lay with one eye open, and no one dared go near the crucifix.

About an hour before day-break the Padre's breathing became so painful that two of the men got behind him and lifted his pillows. The women whispered that his face was changing, and they brought their candles nearer, kneeling close beside his bed. His eyes were alive and had perception in them. He rolled his head to one side and lay looking intently down into the candle-light, without blinking, while his features sharpened. Several times his lips twitched back over his teeth. The watchers held their breath, feeling sure that he would speak before he passed,—and he did. After a facial spasm that was like a sardonic smile, and a clicking of breath in his mouth, their Padre spoke like a horse for the last time:

"*Comete tu cola, Martínez, comete tu cola!*" (Eat your tail, Martínez, eat your tail!) Almost at once he died in a convulsion.

After day-break Trinidad went forth declaring (and the Mexican women confirmed him) that at the moment of death Father Lucero had looked into the other world and beheld Padre Martínez in torment. As long as the Christians who were about that death-bed lived, the story was whispered in Arroyo Hondo.

When the floor of the priest's house was taken up, according to his last instructions, people came from as far as Taos and Santa Cruz and Mora to see the buckskin bags of gold and silver coin that were buried beneath it. Spanish coins, French, American, English, some of them very old. When it was at length conveyed to a Government mint and examined, it was valued at nearly twenty thousand dollars in American money. A great sum for one old priest to have scraped together in a country parish down at the bottom of a ditch.

Book Six

Doña Isabella

1
Don Antonio

Bishop Latour had one very keen worldly ambition; to build in Santa Fé a cathedral which would be worthy of a setting naturally beautiful. As he cherished this wish and meditated upon it, he came to feel that such a building might be a continuation of himself and his purpose, a physical body full of his aspirations after he had passed from the scene. Early in his administration he began setting aside something from his meagre resources for a cathedral fund. In this he was assisted by certain of the rich Mexican *rancheros*, but by no one so much as by Don Antonio Olivares.

Antonio Olivares was the most intelligent and prosperous member of a large family of brothers and cousins, and he was for that time and place a man of wide experience, a man of the world. He had spent the greater part of his life in New Orleans and El Paso del Norte, but he returned to live in Santa Fé several years after Bishop Latour took up his duties there. He brought with him his American wife and a wagon train of furniture, and settled down to spend his declining years in the old ranch house just east of the town where he was born and had grown up. He was then a man of sixty. In early manhood he had lost his first wife; after he went to New Orleans he had married a second time, a Kentucky girl who had grown up among her relatives in Louisiana. She was pretty and accomplished, had been educated at a French convent, and had done much to Europeanize her husband. The refinement of his dress and manners, and his lavish style of living, provoked half-contemptuous envy among his brothers and their friends.

Olivares's wife, Doña Isabella, was a devout Catholic, and at their house the French priests were always welcome and were most cordially entertained. The Señora Olivares had made a pleasant place of the rambling adobe building, with its great court-yard and gateway, carved joists and beams, fine herring-bone ceilings and snug fire-places. She was a gracious hostess, and though no longer very young, she was still attractive to the eye; a slight woman, spirited, quick in movement, with a delicate blonde complexion which she had successfully guarded in trying climates, and fair hair—a little silvered, and perhaps worn in too many puffs and ringlets for the sharpening outline of her face. She spoke French well, Spanish lamely, played the harp, and sang agreeably.

Certainly it was a great piece of luck for Father Latour and Father Vaillant, who lived so much among peons and Indians and rough frontiersmen, to be able to converse in their own tongue now and then with a cultivated woman; to sit by that hospitable fireside, in rooms enriched by old mirrors and engravings and upholstered chairs, where the windows had clean curtains, and the sideboard and cupboards were stocked with plate and Belgian glass. It was refreshing to spend an evening with a couple who were interested in what was going on in the outside world, to eat a good dinner and drink good wine, and listen to music. Father Joseph, that man of inconsistencies, had a pleasing tenor voice, true though not strong. Madame Olivares liked to sing old French songs with him. She was a trifle vain, it must be owned, and when she sang at all, insisted upon singing in three languages, never forgetting her husband's favourites, "La Paloma" and "La Golondrina," and "My Nelly Was A Lady." The Negro melodies of Stephen Foster had already travelled to the frontier, going along the river highways, not in print, but passed on from one humble singer to another.

Don Antonio was a large man, heavy, full at the belt, a trifle bald, and very slow of speech. But his eyes were lively, and the yellow spark in them was often most perceptible when he was quite silent. It was interesting to observe him after dinner, settled in one of his big chairs from New Orleans, a cigar between his long golden-brown fingers, watching his wife at her harp.

There was gossip about the lady in Santa Fé, of course, since she had retained her beautiful complexion and her husband's devoted regard for so many years. The Americans and the Olivares brothers said she dressed much too youthfully, which was perhaps true, and that she had lovers in New Orleans and El Paso del Norte. Her nephews-in-law went so far as to declare that she was enamoured of the Mexican boy the Olivares had brought up from San Antonio to play the banjo for them,—they both loved music, and this boy, Pablo, was a magician with his instrument. All sorts of stories went out from the kitchen; that Doña Isabella had a whole chamber full of dresses so grand that she never wore them here at all; that she took gold from her husband's pockets and hid it under the floor of her room; that she gave him love potions and herb-teas to increase his ardour. This gossip did not mean that her servants were disloyal, but rather that they were proud of their mistress.

Olivares, who read the newspapers, though they were weeks old when he got them, who liked cigars better than cigarettes, and French wine better than whisky, had little in common with his younger brothers. Next to his old friend Manuel Chavez, the two French priests were the men in Santa Fé whose company he most enjoyed, and he let them see it. He was a man who cherished his friends. He liked to call at the Bishop's house to advise him about the care of his young orchard, or to leave a bottle of home-made cherry brandy for Father Joseph. It was Olivares who presented Father Latour with the silver hand-basin and pitcher and toilet accessories which gave him so much satisfaction all the rest of his life. There were good silversmiths among the Mexicans of Santa Fé, and Don Antonio had his own toilet-set copied in hammered silver for his friend. Doña Isabella once remarked that her husband always gave Father Vaillant something good for the palate, and Father Latour something good for the eye.

This couple had one child, a daughter, the Señorita Inez, born long ago and still unmarried. Indeed, it was generally understood that she would never marry. Though she had not taken the veil, her life was that of a nun. She was very plain and had none of her mother's social graces, but she had a beautiful contralto voice. She sang in the Cathedral choir in New Orleans, and taught singing in a convent there. She came to visit her parents only once after they settled in Santa Fé, and she was a somewhat sombre figure in that convivial household. Doña Isabella seemed devotedly attached to her, but afraid of displeasing her. While Inez was there, her mother dressed very plainly, pinned back the little curls that hung over her right ear, and the two women went to church together all day long.

Antonio Olivares was deeply interested in the Bishop's dream of a cathedral. For one thing, he saw that Father Latour had set his heart on building one, and Olivares was the sort of man who liked to help a friend accomplish the desire of his heart. Furthermore, he had a deep affection for his native town, he had travelled and seen fine churches, and he wished there might some day be one in Santa Fé. Many a night he and Father Latour talked of it by the fire; discussed the site, the design, the building stone, the cost and the grave difficulties of raising money. It was the Bishop's hope to begin work upon the building in 1860, ten years after his appointment to the Bishopric. One night, at a long-remembered New Year's party in his house, Olivares announced in the presence of his guests that before the new year was gone he meant to give to the Cathedral fund a sum sufficient to enable Father Latour to carry out his purpose.

That supper party at the Olivares's was memorable because of this pledge, and because it marked a parting of old friends. Doña Isabella was entertaining the officers at the Post, two of whom had received orders to leave Santa Fé. The popular Commandant was called back to Washington, the young lieutenant of cavalry, an Irish Catholic, lately married and very dear to Father Latour, was to be sent farther west. (Before the next New Year's Day came round he was killed in Indian warfare on the plains of Arizona.)

But that night the future troubled nobody; the house was full of light and music, the air warm with that simple hospitality of the frontier, where people dwell in exile, far from their kindred, where they lead rough lives and seldom meet together for pleasure. Kit Carson, who greatly admired Madame Olivares, had come the two days' journey from Taos to be present that night, and brought along his gentle half-breed daughter, lately home from a convent school in St. Louis. On this occasion he wore a handsome buckskin coat, embroidered in silver, with brown velvet cuffs and collar. The officers from the Fort were in dress uniform, the host as usual wore a broadcloth frock-coat. His wife was in a hoop-skirt, a French dress from New Orleans, all covered with little garlands of pink satin roses. The military ladies came out to the Olivares place in an army wagon, to keep their satin shoes from the mud. The Bishop had put on his violet vest, which he seldom wore, and Father Vaillant had donned a fresh new cassock, made by the loving hands of his sister Philomène, in Riom.

Father Latour had used to feel a little ashamed that Joseph kept his sister and her nuns so busy making cassocks and vestments for him; but the last time he was in France he came to see all this in another light. When he was visiting Mother Philomène's convent, one of the younger Sisters had confided to him what an inspiration it was to them, living in retirement, to work for the faraway missions. She told him also how precious to them were Father Vaillant's long letters, letters in which he told his sister of the country, the Indians, the pious Mexican women, the Spanish martyrs of old. These letters, she said, Mother Philomène read aloud in the evening. The nun took Father Latour to a window that jutted out and looked up the narrow street to where the wall turned at an angle, cutting off further view. "Look," she said, "after the Mother has read us one of those letters from her brother, I come and stand in this alcove and look up our little street with its one lamp, and just beyond the turn there, is New Mexico; all that he has written us of those red deserts and blue mountains, the great plains and the herds of bison, and the canyons more profound than our deepest mountain gorges. I can feel that I am there, my heart beats faster, and it seems but a moment until the retiring-bell cuts short my dreams." The Bishop went away believing that it was good for these Sisters to work for Father Joseph.

To-night, when Madame Olivares was complimenting Father Vaillant on the sheen of his poplin and velvet, for some reason Father Latour recalled that moment with the nun in her alcove window, her white face, her burning eyes, and sighed.

After supper was over and the toasts had been drunk, the boy Pablo was called in to play for the company while the gentlemen smoked. The banjo always remained a foreign instrument to Father Latour; he found it more than a little savage. When this strange yellow boy played it, there was softness and languor in the wire strings—but there was also a kind of madness; the recklessness, the call of wild countries which all these men had felt and followed in one way or another. Through clouds of cigar smoke, the scout and the soldiers, the Mexican *rancheros* and the priests, sat silently watching the bent head and crouching shoulders of the banjo player, and his seesawing yellow hand, which sometimes lost all form and became a mere whirl of matter in motion, like a patch of sand-storm.

Observing them thus in repose, in the act of reflection, Father Latour was thinking how each of these men not only had a story, but seemed to have become his story. Those anxious, far-seeing blue eyes of Carson's, to whom could they belong but to a scout and trail-breaker? Don Manuel Chavez, the handsomest man of the company, very elegant in velvet and broadcloth, with delicately cut, disdainful features,—one had only to see him cross the room, or to sit next him at dinner, to feel the electric quality under his cold reserve; the fierceness of some embitterment, the passion for danger.

Chavez boasted his descent from two Castilian knights who freed the city of Chavez from the Moors in 1160. He had estates in the Pecos and in the San Mateo mountains, and a house in Santa Fé, where he hid himself behind his beautiful trees and gardens. He loved the natural beauties of his country with a passion, and he hated the Americans who were blind to them. He was jealous of Carson's fame as an Indian-fighter, declaring that he had seen more Indian warfare before he was twenty than Carson would ever see. He was easily Carson's rival as a pistol shot. With the bow and arrow he had no rival; he had never been beaten. No Indian had ever been known to shoot an arrow as far as Chavez. Every year parties of Indians came up to the Villa to shoot with him for wagers. His house and stables were full of trophies. He took a cool pleasure in stripping the Indians of their horses or silver or blankets, or whatever they had put up on their man. He was proud of his skill with Indian weapons; he had acquired it in a hard school.

When he was a lad of sixteen Manuel Chavez had gone out with a party of Mexican youths to hunt Navajos. In those days, before the American occupation, "hunting Navajos" needed no pretext, it was a form of sport. A company of Mexicans would ride west to the Navajo country, raid a few sheep camps, and come home bringing flocks and ponies and a bunch of prisoners, for every one of whom they received a large bounty from the Mexican Government. It was with such a raiding party that the boy Chavez went out for spoil and adventure.

Finding no Indians abroad, the young Mexicans pushed on farther than they had intended. They did not know that it was the season when all the roving Navajo bands gather at the Canyon de Chelly for their religious ceremonies, and they rode on impetuously until they came out upon the rim of that mysterious and terrifying canyon itself, then swarming with Indians. They were immediately surrounded, and retreat was impossible. They fought on the naked sandstone ledges that overhang that gulf. Don José Chavez, Manuel's older brother, was captain of the party, and was one of the first to fall. The company of fifty were slaughtered to a man. Manuel was the fifty-first, and he survived. With seven arrow wounds, and one shaft clear through his body, he was left for dead in a pile of corpses.

That night, while the Navajos were celebrating their victory, the boy crawled along the rocks until he had high boulders between him and the enemy, and then started eastward on foot. It was summer, and the heat of that red sandstone country is intense. His wounds were on fire. But he had the superb vitality of early youth. He walked for two days and nights without finding a drop of water, covering a distance of sixty odd miles, across the plain, across the mountain, until he came to the famous spring on the other side, where Fort Defiance was afterward built. There he drank and bathed his wounds and slept. He had had no food since the morning before the fight; near the spring he found some large cactus plants, and slicing away the spines with his hunting-knife, he filled his stomach with the juicy pulp.

From here, still without meeting a human creature, he stumbled on until he reached the San Mateo mountain, north of Laguna. In a mountain valley he came upon a camp of Mexican shepherds, and fell unconscious. The shepherds made a litter of saplings and their sheepskin coats and carried him into the village of Cebolleta, where he lay delirious for many days. Years afterward, when Chavez came into his inheritance, he bought that beautiful valley in the San Mateo mountain where he had sunk unconscious under two noble oak trees. He built a house between those twin oaks, and made a fine estate there.

Never reconciled to American rule, Chavez lived in seclusion when he was in Santa Fé. At the first rumour of an Indian outbreak, near or far, he rode off to add a few more scalps to his record. He distrusted the new Bishop because of his friendliness toward Indians and Yankees. Besides, Chavez was a Martínez man. He had come here to-night only in compliment to Señora Olivares; he hated to spend an evening among American uniforms.

When the banjo player was exhausted, Father Joseph said that as for him, he would like a little drawing-room music, and he led Madame Olivares to her harp. She was very charming at her instrument; the pose suited her tip-tilted canary head, and her little foot and white arms.

This was the last time the Bishop heard her sing "La Paloma" for her admiring husband, whose eyes smiled at her even when his heavy face seemed asleep.

O livares died on Septuagesima Sunday—fell over by his own fire-place when he was lighting the candles after supper, and the banjo boy was sent running for the Bishop. Before midnight two of the Olivares brothers, half drunk with brandy and excitement, galloped out of Santa Fé, on the road to Albuquerque, to employ an American lawyer.

2
The Lady

Antonio Olivares's funeral was the most solemn and magnificent ever seen in Santa Fé, but Father Vaillant was not there. He was off on a long missionary journey to the south, and did not reach home until Madame Olivares had been a widow for some weeks. He had scarcely got off his riding-boots when he was called into Father Latour's study to see her lawyer.

Olivares had entrusted the management of his affairs to a young Irish Catholic, Boyd O'Reilly, who had come out from Boston to practise law in the new Territory. There were no steel safes in Santa Fé at that time, but O'Reilly had kept Olivares's will in his strong-box. The document was brief and clear: Antonio's estate amounted to about two hundred thousand dollars in American money (a considerable fortune in those days). The income therefrom was to be enjoyed by "my wife, Isabella Olivares, and her daughter, Inez Olivares," during their lives, and after their decease his property was to go to the Church, to the Society for the Propagation of the Faith. The codicil, in favour of the Cathedral fund, had, unfortunately, never been added to the will.

The young lawyer explained to Father Vaillant that the Olivares brothers had retained the leading legal firm of Albuquerque and were contesting the will. Their point of attack was that Señorita Inez was too old to be the daughter of the Señora Olivares. Don Antonio had been a promiscuous lover in his young days, and his brothers held that Inez was the offspring of some temporary attachment, and had been adopted by Doña Isabella. O'Reilly had sent to new Orleans for an attested copy of the marriage record of the Olivares couple, and the birth certificate of Señorita Inez. But in Kentucky, where the Señora was born, no birth records were kept; there was no document to prove the age of Isabella Olivares, and she could not be persuaded to admit her true age. It was generally believed in Santa Fé that she was still in her early forties, in which case she would not have been more than six or eight years old at the date when Inez was born. In reality the lady was past fifty, but when O'Reilly had tried to persuade her to admit this in court, she simply refused to listen to him. He begged the Bishop and the Vicar to use their influence with her to this end.

Father Latour shrank from interfering in so delicate a matter, but Father Vaillant saw at once that it was their plain duty to protect the two women and, at the same time, secure the rights of the Propaganda. Without more ado he threw on his old cloak over his cassock, and the three men set off through the red mud to the Olivares' hacienda in the hills east of the town.

Father Joseph had not been to the Olivares's house since the night of the New Year's party, and he sighed as he approached the place, already transformed by neglect. The big gate was propped open by a pole because the iron hook was gone, the court-yard was littered with rags and meat bones which the dogs had carried there and no one had taken away. The big parrot cage, hanging in the *portale,* was filthy, and the birds were squalling. When O'Reilly rang the bell at the outer gate, Pablo, the banjo player, came running out with tousled hair and a dirty shirt to admit the visitors. He took them into the long living-room, which was empty and cold, the fire-place dark, the hearth unswept. Chairs and window-sills were deep in red dust, the glass panes dirty, and streaked as if by teardrops. On the writing-table were empty bottles and sticky glasses and cigar ends. In one corner stood the harp in its green cover.

Pablo asked the Fathers to be seated. His mistress was staying in bed, he said, and the cook had burnt her hand, and the other maids were lazy. He brought wood and laid a fire.

After some time, Doña Isabella entered, dressed in heavy mourning, her face very white against the black, and her eyes red. The curls about her neck and ears were pale, too—quite ashen.

After Father Vaillant had greeted her and spoken consoling words, the young lawyer began once more gently to explain to her the difficulties that confronted them, and what they must do to defeat the action of the Olivares family. She sat submissively, touching her eyes and nose with her little lace handkerchief, and clearly not even trying to understand a word of what he said to her.

Father Joseph soon lost patience and himself approached the widow. "You understand, my child," he began briskly, "that your husband's brothers are determined to disregard his wishes, to defraud you and your daughter, and, eventually, the Church. This is no time for childish vanity. To prevent this outrage to your husband's memory, you must satisfy the court that you are old enough to be the mother of Mademoiselle Inez. You must resolutely declare your true age; fifty-three, is it not?"

Doña Isabella became pallid with fright. She shrank into one end of the deep sofa, but her blue eyes focused and gathered light, as she became intensely, rigidly animated in her corner,—her back against the wall, as it were.

"Fifty-three!" she cried in a voice of horrified amazement. "Why, I never heard of anything so outrageous! I was forty-two my last birthday. It was in December, the fourth of December. If Antonio were here, he would tell you! And he wouldn't let you scold me and talk about business to me, either,

Father Joseph. He never let anybody talk about business to me!" She hid her face in her little handkerchief and began to cry.

Father Latour checked his impetuous Vicar, and sat down on the sofa beside Madame Olivares, feeling very sorry for her and speaking very gently. "Forty-two to your friends, dear Madame Olivares, and to the world. In heart and face you are younger than that. But to the Law and the Church there must be a literal reckoning. A formal statement in court will not make you any older to your friends; it will not add one line to your face. A woman, you know, is as old as she looks."

"That's very sweet of you to say, Bishop Latour," the lady quavered, looking up at him with tear-bright eyes. "But I never could hold up my head again. Let the Olivares have that old money. I don't want it."

Father Vaillant sprang up and glared down at her as if he could put common sense into her drooping head by the mere intensity of his gaze. "Four hundred thousand pesos, Señora Isabella!" he cried. "Ease and comfort for you and your daughter all the rest of your lives. Would you make your daughter a beggar? The Olivares will take everything."

"I can't help it about Inez," she pleaded. "Inez means to go into the convent anyway. And I don't care about the money. *Ah, mon père, je voudrais mieux être jeune et mendiante, que n'être que vieille et riche, certes, oui!*"

Father Joseph caught her icy cold hand. "And have you a right to defraud the Church of what is left to it in your trust? Have you thought of the consequences to yourself of such a betrayal?"

Father Latour glanced sternly at his Vicar. "*Assez*," he said quietly. He took the little hand Father Joseph had released and bent over it, kissing it respectfully. "We must not press this any further. We must leave this to Madame Olivares and her own conscience. I believe, my daughter, you will come to realize that this sacrifice of your vanity would be for your soul's peace. Looking merely at the temporal aspect of the case, you would find poverty hard to bear. You would have to live upon the Olivares's charity, would you not? I do not wish to see this come about. I have a selfish interest; I wish you to be always your charming self and to make a little *poésie* in life for us here. We have not much of that."

Madame Olivares stopped crying. She raised her head and sat drying her eyes. Suddenly she took hold of one of the buttons on the Bishop's cassock and began twisting it with nervous fingers.

"Father," she said timidly, "what is the youngest I could possibly be, to be Inez's mother?"

The Bishop could not pronounce the verdict; he hesitated, flushed, then passed it on to O'Reilly with an open gesture of his fine white hand.

"Fifty-two, Señora Olivares," said the young man respectfully. "If I can get you to admit that, and stick to it, I feel sure we will win our case."

"Very well, Mr. O'Reilly." She bowed her head. As her visitors rose, she sat looking down at the dust-covered rugs. "Before everybody!" she murmured, as if to herself.

When they were tramping home, Father Joseph said that, as for him, he would rather combat the superstitions of a whole Indian pueblo than the vanity of one white woman.

"And I would rather do almost anything than go through such a scene again," said the Bishop with a frown. "I don't think I ever assisted at anything so cruel."

Boyd O'Reilly defeated the Olivares brothers and won his case. The Bishop would not go to the court hearing, but Father Vaillant was there, standing in the malodorous crowd (there were no chairs in the court room), and his knees shook under him when the young lawyer, with the fierceness born of fright, poked his finger at his client and said:

"Señora Olivares, you are fifty-two years of age, are you not?"

Madame Olivares was swathed in mourning, her face a streak of shadowed white between folds of black veil.

"Yes, sir." The crape barely let it through.

The night after the verdict was pronounced, Manuel Chavez, with several of Antonio's old friends, called upon the widow to congratulate her. Word of their intention had gone about the town and put others in the mood to call at a house that had been closed to visitors for so long. A considerable company gathered there that evening, including some of the military people, and several hereditary enemies of the Olivares brothers.

The cook, stimulated by the sight of the long *sala* full of people once more, hastily improvised a supper. Pablo put on a white shirt and a velvet jacket, and began to carry up from the cellar his late master's best whisky and sherry, and quarts of champagne. (The Mexicans are very fond of sparkling wines. Only a few years before this, an American trader who had got into serious political trouble with the Mexican military authorities in Santa Fé, regained their confidence and friendship by presenting them with a large wagon shipment of champagne—three thousand, three hundred and ninety-two bottles, indeed!)

This hospitable mood came upon the house suddenly, nothing had been prepared beforehand. The wine glasses were full of dust, but Pablo wiped them out with the shirt he had just taken off, and without instructions from anyone he began gliding about with a tray full of glasses, which he afterward refilled many times, taking his station at the sideboard. Even Doña Isabella drank a little champagne; when she had sipped one glass with the young Georgia captain, she could not refuse to take another with their nearest neighbour, Ferdinand Sanchez, always a true friend to her husband. Everyone was gay, the servants and the guests, everything sparkled like a garden after a shower.

Father Latour and Father Vaillant, having heard nothing of this spontaneous gathering of friends, set off at eight o'clock to make a call upon the brave widow. When they entered the court-yard, they were astonished to hear music within, and to see light streaming from the long row of windows behind the *portale*. Without stopping to knock, they opened the door into the *sala*. Many candles were burning. Señors were standing about in long frock-coats buttoned over full figures. O'Reilly and a group of officers from the Fort surrounded the sideboard, where Pablo, with a white napkin wrapped showily about his wrist, was pouring champagne. From the other end of the room sounded the high tinkle of the harp, and Doña Isabella's voice:

> *"Listen to the mocking-bird,*
> *Listen to the mocking-bird!"*

The priests waited in the doorway until the song was finished, then went forward to pay their respects to the hostess. She was wearing the unrelieved white that grief permitted, and the yellow curls were bobbing as of old—three behind her right ear, one over either temple, and a little row across the back of her neck. As she saw the two black figures approaching, she dropped her arms from the harp, took her satin toe from the pedal, and rose, holding out a hand to each. Her eyes were bright, and her face beamed with affection for her spiritual fathers. But her greeting was a playful reproach, uttered loud enough to be heard above the murmur of conversing groups:

"I never shall forgive you, Father Joseph, nor you either, Bishop Latour, for that awful lie you made me tell in court about my age!"

The two churchmen bowed amid laughter and applause.

BOOK SEVEN

The Great Diocese

1
The Month of Mary

The Bishop's work was sometimes assisted, often impeded, by external events.

By the Gadsden Purchase, executed three years after Father Latour came to Santa Fé, the United States took over from Mexico a great territory which now forms southern New Mexico and Arizona. The authorities at Rome notified Father Latour that this new territory was to be annexed to his diocese, but that as the national boundary lines often cut parishes in two, the boundaries of Church jurisdiction must be settled by conference with the Mexican Bishops of Chihuahua and Sonora. Such conferences would necessitate a journey of nearly four thousand miles. As Father Vaillant remarked, at Rome they did not seem to realize that it was no easy matter for two missionaries on horseback to keep up with the march of history.

The question hung fire for some years, the subject of voluminous correspondence. At last, in 1858, Father Vaillant was sent to arrange the debated boundaries with the Mexican Bishops. He started in the autumn and spent the whole winter on the road, going from El Paso del Norte west to Tucson, on to Santa Magdalena and Guaymas, a seaport town on the gulf of California, and did some seafaring on the Pacific before he turned homeward.

On his return trip he was stricken with malarial fever, resulting from exposure and bad water, and lay seriously ill in a cactus desert in Arizona. Word of his illness came to Santa Fé by an Indian runner, and Father Latour and Jacinto rode across New Mexico and half of Arizona, found Father Vaillant, and brought him back by easy stages.

He was ill in the Bishop's house for two months. This was the first spring that he and Father Latour had both been there at the same time, to enjoy the garden they had laid out soon after they first came to Santa Fé.

It was the month of Mary and the month of May. Father Vaillant was lying on an army cot, covered with blankets, under the grape arbour in the garden, watching the Bishop and his gardener at work in the vegetable plots. The apple trees were in blossom, the cherry blooms had gone by. The air and the earth interpenetrated in the warm gusts of spring; the soil was full of sunlight, and the sunlight full of red dust. The air one breathed was saturated with earthy smells, and the grass under foot had a reflection of blue sky in it.

This garden had been laid out six years ago, when the Bishop brought his fruit trees (then dry switches) up from St. Louis in wagons, along with the blessed Sisters of Loretto, who came to found the Academy of Our Lady of Light. The school was now well established, reckoned a benefit to the community by Protestants as well as Catholics, and the trees were bearing. Cuttings from them were already yielding fruit in many Mexican gardens. While the Bishop was away on that first trip to Baltimore, Father Joseph had, in addition to his many official duties, found time to instruct their Mexican housekeeper, Fructosa, in cookery. Later Bishop Latour took in hand Fructosa's husband, Tranquilino, and trained him as a gardener. They had boldly planned for the future; the ground behind the church, between the Bishop's house and the Academy, they laid out as a spacious orchard and kitchen-garden. Ever since then the Bishop had worked on it, planting and pruning. It was his only recreation.

A line of young poplars linked the Episcopal courtyard with the school. On the south, against the earth wall, was the one row of trees they had found growing there when they first came,—old, old tamarisks, with twisted trunks. They had been so neglected, left to fight for life in such hard, sun-baked, burro-trodden ground, that their trunks had the hardness of cypress. They looked, indeed, like very old posts, well seasoned and polished by time, miraculously endowed with the power to burst into delicate foliage and flowers, to cover themselves with long brooms of lavender-pink blossom.

Father Joseph had come to love the tamarisk above all trees. It had been the companion of his wanderings. All along his way through the deserts of New Mexico and Arizona, wherever he had come upon a Mexican homestead, out of the sun-baked earth, against the sun-baked adobe walls, the tamarisk waved its feathery plumes of bluish green. The family burro was tied to its trunk, the chickens scratched under it, the dogs slept in its shade, the washing was hung on its branches. Father Latour had often remarked that this tree seemed especially designed in shape and colour for the adobe village. The sprays of bloom which adorn it are merely another shade of the red earth walls, and its fibrous trunk is full of gold and lavender tints. Father Joseph respected the Bishop's eye for such things, but himself he loved it merely because it was the tree of the people, and was like one of the family in every Mexican household.

This was a very happy season for Father Vaillant. For years he had not been able properly to observe this month which in his boyhood he had selected to be the holy month of the year for him, dedicated to the contemplation of his Gracious Patroness. In his former missionary life, on the Great Lakes, he used always to go into retreat at this season. But here there was no time for such things. Last year, in May, he had been on his way to the Hopi Indians, riding thirty miles a day; marrying, baptizing, confessing as he went, making camp in the sand-hills at night. His devotions had been constantly interrupted by practical considerations.

But this year, because of his illness, the month of Mary he had been able to give to Mary; to Her he had consecrated his waking hours. At night he sank to sleep with the sense of Her protection. In the morning when he awoke, before he had opened his eyes, he was conscious of a special sweetness in the air,—Mary, and the month of May. *Alma Mater redemptoris!* Once more he had been able to worship with the ardour of a young religious, for whom religion is pure personal devotion, unalloyed by expediency and the benumbing cares of a missionary's work. Once again this had been his month; his Patroness had given it to him, the season that had always meant so much in his religious life.

He smiled to remember a time long ago, when he was a young curate in Cendre, in the Puy-de-Dôme; how he had planned a season of special devotion to the Blessed Virgin for May, and how the old priest to whom he was assistant had blasted his hopes by cold disapproval. The old man had come through the Terror, had been trained in the austerity of those days of the persecution of the clergy, and he was not untouched by Jansenism. Young Father Joseph bore his rebuke with meekness, and went sadly to his own chamber. There he took his rosary and spent the entire day in prayer. "*Not according to my desires, but if it is for thy glory, grant me this boon, O Mary, my hope.*" In the evening of that same day the old pastor sent for him, and unsolicited granted him the request he had so sternly denied in the morning. How joyfully Father Joseph had written all this to his sister Philomène, then a pupil with the nuns of the Visitation in their native Riom, begging her to make him a quantity of artificial flowers for his May altar. How richly she had responded!—and she rejoiced no less than he that his May devotions were so largely attended, especially by the young people of the parish, in whom a notable increase of piety was manifest. Father Vaillant's had been a close-knit family—losing their mother while they were yet children had brought the brothers and sisters the closer together—and with this sister, Philomène, he had shared all his hopes and desires and his deepest religious life.

Ever since then, all the most important events in his own history had occurred in the blessed month when this sinful and sullied world puts on white as if to commemorate the Annunciation, and become, for a little, lovely enough to be in truth the Bride of Christ. It was in May that he had been given grace to perform the hardest act of his life; to leave his country, to part from his dear sister and his father (under what sad circumstances!), and to start for the New World to take up a missionary's labours. That parting was not a parting, but an escape—a running away, a betrayal of family trust for the sake of a higher trust. He could smile at it now, but at the time it had been terrible enough. The Bishop, thinning carrots yonder, would remember. It was because of what Father Latour had been to him in that hour, indeed, that Father Joseph was here in a garden in Santa Fé. He would never have left his dear Sandusky when the newly appointed Bishop asked him to share his hardships, had he not said to himself: "Ah, now it is he who is torn by perplexity! I will be to him now what he was to me that day when we stood by the road-side, waiting for the *diligence* to Paris, and my purpose broke, and,—he saved me."

That time came back upon Father Vaillant now so keenly that he wiped a little moisture from his eyes,—(he was quickly moved, after the way of sick people) and he cleared his glasses and called:

"Father Latour, it is time for you to rest your back. You have been stooping over a great while."

The Bishop came and sat down in a wheelbarrow that stood at the edge of the arbour.

"I have been thinking that I shall no longer pray for your speedy recovery, Joseph. The only way I can keep my Vicar within call is to have him sick."

Father Joseph smiled.

"You are not in Santa Fé a great deal yourself, my Bishop."

"Well, I shall be here this summer, and I hope to keep you with me. This year I want you to see my lotus flowers. Tranquilino will let the water into my lake this afternoon." The lake was a little pond in the middle of the garden, into which Tranquilino, clever with water, like all Mexicans, had piped a stream from the Santa Fé creek flowing near at hand. "Last summer, while you were away," the Bishop continued, "we had more than a hundred lotus blossoms floating on that little lake. And all from five bulbs that I put into my valise in Rome."

"When do they blossom?"

"They begin in June, but they are at their best in July."

"Then you must hurry them up a little. For with my Bishop's permission, I shall be gone in July."

"So soon? And why?"

Father Vaillant moved uneasily under his blankets. "To hunt for lost Catholics, Jean! Utterly lost Catholics, down in your new territory, towards Tucson. There are hundreds of poor families down there who have never seen a priest. I want to go from house to house this time, to every little settlement. They are full of devotion and faith, and it has nothing to feed upon but the most mistaken superstitions. They remember their prayers all wrong. They cannot read, and since there is no one to instruct them, how can they get right? They are like seeds, full of germination but with no moisture. A mere contact is enough to make them a living part of the Church. The more I work with the Mexicans, the more I believe it was people like them our

Saviour bore in mind when He said, *Unless ye become as little children*. He was thinking of people who are not clever in the things of this world, whose minds are not upon gain and worldly advancement. These poor Christians are not thrifty like our country people at home; they have no veneration for property, no sense of material values. I stop a few hours in a village, I administer the sacraments and hear confessions, I leave in every house some little token, a rosary or a religious picture, and I go away feeling that I have conferred immeasurable happiness, and have released faithful souls that were shut away from God by neglect.

"Down near Tucson a Pima Indian convert once asked me to go off into the desert with him, as he had something to show me. He took me into a place so wild that a man less accustomed to these things might have mistrusted and feared for his life. We descended into a terrifying canyon of black rock, and there in the depths of a cave, he showed me a golden chalice, vestments and cruets, all the paraphernalia for celebrating Mass. His ancestors had hidden these sacred objects there when the mission was sacked by Apaches, he did not know how many generations ago. The secret had been handed down in his family, and I was the first priest who had ever come to restore to God his own. To me, that is the situation in a parable. The Faith, in that wild frontier, is like a buried treasure; they guard it, but they do not know how to use it to their soul's salvation. A word, a prayer, a service, is all that is needed to set free those souls in bondage. I confess I am covetous of that mission. I desire to be the man who restores these lost children to God. It will be the greatest happiness of my life."

The Bishop did not reply at once to this appeal. At last he said gravely, "You must realize that I have need of you here, Father Joseph. My duties are too many for one man."

"But you do not need me so much as they do!" Father Joseph threw off his coverings and sat up in his cassock, putting his feet to the ground. "Any one of our good French priests from Montferrand can serve you here. It is work that can be done by intelligence. But down there it is work for the heart, for a particular sympathy, and none of our new priests understand those poor natures as I do. I have almost become a Mexican! I have learned to like *chili colorado* and mutton fat. Their foolish ways no longer offend me, their very faults are dear to me. I am *their man!*"

"Ah, no doubt, no doubt! But I must insist upon your lying down for the present."

Father Vaillant, flushed and excited, dropped back upon his pillows, and the Bishop took a short turn through the garden,—to the row of tamarisk trees and back. He walked slowly, with even, unhesitating pace, with that slender, unrigid erectness, and the fine carriage of head, which always made him seem master of the situation. No one would have guessed that a sharp struggle was going on within him. Father Joseph's impassioned request had spoiled a cherished plan, and brought Father Latour a bitter personal disappointment. There was but one thing to do,—and before he reached the tamarisks he had done it. He broke off a spray of the dry lilac-coloured flowers to punctuate and seal, as it were, his renunciation. He returned with the same easy, deliberate tread, and stood smiling beside the army cot.

"Your feeling must be your guide in this matter, Joseph. I shall put no obstacles in your way. A certain care for your health I must insist upon, but when you are quite well, you must follow the duty that calls loudest."

They were both silent for a few moments. Father Joseph closed his eyes against the sunlight, and Father Latour stood lost in thought, drawing the plume of tamarisk blossom absently through his delicate, rather nervous fingers. His hands had a curious authority, but not the calmness so often seen in the hands of priests; they seemed always to be investigating and making firm decisions.

The two friends were roused from their reflections by a frantic beating of wings. A bright flock of pigeons swept over their heads to the far end of the garden, where a woman was just emerging from the gate that led into the school grounds; Magdalena, who came every day to feed the doves and to gather flowers. The Sisters had given her charge of the altar decoration of the school chapel for this month, and she came for the Bishop's apple blossoms and daffodils. She advanced in a whirlwind of gleaming wings, and Tranquilino dropped his spade and stood watching her. At one moment the whole flock of doves caught the light in such a way that they all became invisible at once, dissolved in light and disappeared as salt dissolves in water. The next moment they flashed around, black and silver against the sun. They settled upon Magdalena's arms and shoulders, ate from her hand. When she put a crust of bread between her lips, two doves hung in the air before her face, stirring their wings and pecking at the morsel. A handsome woman she had grown to be, with her comely figure and the deep claret colour under the golden brown of her cheeks.

"Who would think, to look at her now, that we took her from a place where every vileness of cruelty and lust was practised!" murmured Father Vaillant. "Not since the days of early Christianity has the Church been able to do what it can here."

"She is but twenty-seven or -eight years old. I wonder whether she ought not to marry again," said the Bishop thoughtfully. "Though she seems so contented, I have sometimes surprised a tragic shadow in her eyes. Do you remember the terrible look in her eyes when we first saw her?"

"Can I ever forget it! But her very body has changed. She was then a shapeless, cringing creature. I thought her half-witted. No, no! She has had enough of the storms of this world. Here she is safe and happy." Father Vaillant sat up and called to her. "Magdalena, Magdalena, my child, come here and talk to us for a little. Two men grow lonely when they see nobody but each other."

2
December Night

Father Vaillant had been absent in Arizona since midsummer, and it was now December. Bishop Latour had been going through one of those periods of coldness and doubt which, from his boyhood, had occasionally settled down upon his spirit and made him feel an alien, wherever he was. He attended to his correspondence, went on his rounds among the parish priests, held services at missions that were without pastors, superintended the building of the addition to the Sisters' school: but his heart was not in these things.

One night about three weeks before Christmas he was lying in his bed, unable to sleep, with the sense of failure clutching at his heart. His prayers were empty words and brought him no refreshment. His soul had become a barren field. He had nothing within himself to give his priests or his people. His work seemed superficial, a house built upon the sands. His great diocese was still a heathen country. The Indians travelled their old road of fear and darkness, battling with evil omens and ancient shadows. The Mexicans were children who played with their religion.

As the night wore on, the bed on which the Bishop lay became a bed of thorns; he could bear it no longer. Getting up in the dark, he looked out of the window and was surprised to find that it was snowing, that the ground was already lightly covered. The full moon, hidden by veils of cloud, threw a pale phosphorescent luminousness over the heavens, and the towers of the church stood up black against this silvery fleece. Father Latour felt a longing to go into the church to pray; but instead he lay down again under his blankets. Then, realizing that it was the cold of the church he shrank from, and despising himself, he rose again, dressed quickly, and went out into the court, throwing on over his cassock that faithful old cloak that was the twin of Father Vaillant's.

They had bought the cloth for those coats in Paris, long ago, when they were young men staying at the Seminary for Foreign Missions in the rue du Bac, preparing for their first voyage to the New World. The cloth had been made up into caped riding-cloaks by a German tailor in Ohio, and lined with fox fur. Years afterward, when Father Latour was about to start on his long journey in search of his Bishopric, that same tailor had made the cloaks over and relined them with squirrel skins, as more appropriate for a mild climate. These memories and many others went through the Bishop's mind as he wrapped the trusty garment about him and crossed the court to the sacristy, with the big iron key in his hand.

The court was white with snow, and the shadows of walls and buildings stood out sharply in the faint light from the moon muffled in vapour. In the deep doorway of the sacristy he saw a crouching figure—a woman, he made out, and she was weeping bitterly. He raised her up and took her inside. As soon as he had lit a candle, he recognized her, and could have guessed her errand.

It was an old Mexican woman, called Sada, who was slave in an American family. They were Protestants, very hostile to the Roman Church, and they did not allow her to go to Mass or to receive the visits of a priest. She was carefully watched at home,—but in winter, when the heated rooms of the house were desirable to the family, she was put to sleep in a woodshed. Tonight, unable to sleep for the cold, she had gathered courage for this heroic action, had slipped out through the stable door and come running up an alley-way to the House of God to pray. Finding the front doors of the church fastened, she had made her way into the Bishop's garden and come round to the sacristy, only to find that, too, shut against her.

The Bishop stood holding the candle and watching her face while she spoke her few words; a dark brown peon face, worn thin and sharp by life and sorrow. It seemed to him that he had never seen pure goodness shine out of a human countenance as it did from hers. He saw that she had no stockings under her shoes,—the cast-off rawhides of her master,—and beneath her frayed black shawl was only a thin calico dress, covered with patches. Her teeth struck together as she stood trying to control her shivering. With one movement of his free hand the Bishop took the furred cloak from his shoulders and put it about her. This frightened her. She cowered under it, murmuring, "Ah, no, no, Padre!"

"You must obey your Padre, my daughter. Draw that cloak about you, and we will go into the church to pray."

The church was utterly black except for the red spark of the sanctuary lamp before the high altar. Taking her hand, and holding the candle before him, he led her across the choir to the Lady Chapel. There he began to light the tapers before the Virgin. Old Sada fell on her knees and kissed the floor. She kissed the feet of the Holy Mother, the pedestal on which they stood, crying all the while. But from the working of her face, from the beautiful tremors which passed over it, he knew they were tears of ecstasy.

"Nineteen years, Father; nineteen years since I have seen the holy things of the altar!"

"All that is passed, Sada. You have remembered the holy things in your heart. We will pray together."

The Bishop knelt beside her, and they began, *O Holy Mary, Queen of Virgins*. . . .

More than once Father Vaillant had spoken to the Bishop of this aged captive. There had been much whispering among the devout women of the parish about her pitiful case. The Smiths, with whom she lived, were Georgia people, who had at one time lived in El Paso del Norte, and they had taken her back to their native State with them. Not long ago some disgrace had come upon this family in Georgia, they had been forced to sell all their Negro slaves and flee the State. The Mexican woman they could not sell because they had no legal title to her, her position was irregular. Now that they were back in a Mexican country, the Smiths were afraid their charwoman might escape from them and find asylum among her own people, so they kept strict watch upon her. They did not allow her to go outside their own *patio*, not even to accompany her mistress to market.

Two women of the Altar Guild had been so bold as to go into the *patio* to talk with Sada when she was washing clothes, but they had been rudely driven away by the mistress of the house. Mrs. Smith had come running out into the court, half dressed, and told them that if they had business at her *casa* they were to come in by the front door, and not sneak in through the stable to frighten a poor silly creature. When they said they had come to ask Sada to go to Mass with them, she told them she had got the poor creature out of the clutches of the priests once, and would see to it that she did not fall into them again.

Even after that rebuff a very pious neighbour woman had tried to say a word to Sada through the alley door of the stable, where she was unloading wood off the burro. But the old servant had put her finger to her lips and motioned the visitor away, glancing back over her shoulder the while with such an expression of terror that the intruder hastened off, surmising that Sada would be harshly used if she were caught speaking to anyone. The good woman went immediately to Father Vaillant with this story, and he had consulted the Bishop, declaring that something ought to be done to secure the consolations of religion for the bond-woman. But the Bishop replied that the time was not yet; for the present it was inexpedient to antagonize these people. The Smiths were the leaders of a small group of low-caste Protestants who took every occasion to make trouble for the Catholics. They hung about the door of the church on festival days with mockery and loud laughter, spoke insolently to the nuns in the street, stood jeering and blaspheming when the procession went by on Corpus Christi Sunday. There were five sons in the Smith family, fellows of low habits and evil tongues. Even the two younger boys, still children, showed a vicious disposition. Tranquilino had repeatedly driven these two boys out of the Bishop's garden, where they came with their lewd companions to rob the young pear trees or to speak filth against the priests.

When they rose from their knees, Father Latour told Sada he was glad to know that she remembered her prayers so well.

"Ah, Padre, every night I say my Rosary to my Holy Mother, no matter where I sleep!" declared the old creature passionately, looking up into his face and pressing her knotted hands against her breast.

When he asked if she had her beads with her, she was confused. She kept them tied with a cord around her waist, under her clothes, as the only place she could hide them safely.

He spoke soothingly to her. "Remember this, Sada; in the year to come, and during the Novena before Christmas, I will not forget to pray for you whenever I offer the Blessed Sacrifice of the Mass. Be at rest in your heart, for I will remember you in my silent supplications before the altar as I do my own sisters and my nieces."

Never, as he afterward told Father Vaillant, had it been permitted him to behold such deep experience of the holy joy of religion as on that pale December night. He was able to feel, kneeling beside her, the preciousness of the things of the altar to her who was without possessions; the tapers, the image of the Virgin, the figures of the saints, the Cross that took away indignity from suffering and made pain and poverty a means of fellowship with Christ. Kneeling beside the much enduring bond-woman, he experienced those holy mysteries as he had done in his young manhood. He seemed able to feel all it meant to her to know that there was a Kind Woman in Heaven, though there were such cruel ones on earth. Old people, who have felt blows and toil and known the world's hard hand, need, even more than children do, a woman's tenderness. Only a Woman, divine, could know all that a woman can suffer.

Not often, indeed, had Jean Marie Latour come so near to the Fountain of all Pity as in the Lady Chapel that night; the pity that no man born of woman could ever utterly cut himself off from; that was for the murderer on the scaffold, as it was for the dying soldier or the martyr on the rack. The beautiful concept of Mary pierced the priest's heart like a sword.

"*O Sacred Heart of Mary!*" she murmured by his side, and he felt how that name was food and raiment, friend and mother to her. He received the miracle in her heart into his own, saw through her eyes, knew that his poverty was as bleak as hers. When the Kingdom of Heaven had first come into the world, into a cruel world of torture and slaves and masters, He who brought it had said, "*And whosoever is least among you, the same shall be first in the Kingdom of Heaven.*" This church was Sada's house, and he was a servant in it.

The Bishop heard the old woman's confession. He blessed her and put both hands upon her head. When he took her down the nave to let her out of the church, Sada made to lift his cloak from her shoulders. He restrained her, telling her she must keep it for her own, and sleep in it at night. But she slipped out of it hurriedly; such a thought seemed to terrify her. "No, no, Father. If they were to find it on me!" More than that, she did not accuse her oppressors. But as she put it off, she stroked the old garment and patted it as if it were a living thing that had been kind to her.

Happily Father Latour bethought him of a little silver medal, with a figure of the Virgin, he had in his pocket. He gave it to her, telling her that it had been blessed by the Holy Father himself. Now she would have a treasure to hide and guard, to adore while her watchers slept. Ah, he thought, for one who cannot read—or think—the Image, the physical form of Love!

He fitted the great key into its lock, the door swung slowly back on its wooden hinges. The peace without seemed all one with the peace in his own soul. The snow had stopped, the gauzy clouds that had ribbed the arch of heaven were now all sunk into one soft white fog bank over the Sangre de Cristo mountains. The full moon shone high in the blue vault, majestic, lonely, benign. The Bishop stood in the doorway of his church, lost in thought, looking at the line of black footprints his departing visitor had left in the wet scurf of snow.

3
Spring in the Navajo Country

Father Vaillant was away in Arizona all winter. When the first hint of spring was in the air, the Bishop and Jacinto set out on a long ride across New Mexico, to the Painted Desert and the Hopi villages. After they left Oraibi, the Bishop rode several days to the south, to visit a Navajo friend who had lately lost his only son, and who had paid the Bishop the compliment of sending word of the boy's death to him at Santa Fé.

Father Latour had known Eusabio a long while, had met him soon after he first came to his new diocese. The Navajo was in Santa Fé at that time, assisting the military officers to quiet an outbreak of the never-ending quarrel between his people and the Hopis. Ever since then the Bishop and the Indian chief had entertained an increasing regard for each other. Eusabio brought his son all the way to Santa Fé to have the bishop baptize him,—that one beloved son who had died during this last winter.

Though he was ten years younger than Father Latour, Eusabio was one of the most influential men among the Navajo people, and one of the richest in sheep and horses. In Santa Fé and Albuquerque he was respected for his intelligence and authority, and admired for his fine presence. He was extremely tall, even for a Navajo, with a face like a Roman general's of Republican times. He always dressed very elegantly in velvet and buckskin rich with bead and quill embroidery, belted with silver, and wore a blanket of the finest wool and design. His arms, under the loose sleeves of his shirt, were covered with silver bracelets, and on his breast hung very old necklaces of wampum and turquoise and coral—Mediterranean coral, that had been left in the Navajo country by Coronado's captains when they passed through it on their way to discover the Hopi villages and the Grand Canyon.

Eusabio lived, with his relatives and dependents, in a group of hogans on the Colorado Chiquito; to the west and south and north his kinsmen herded his great flocks.

Father Latour and Jacinto arrived at the cluster of booth-like cabins during a high sand-storm, which circled about them and their mules like snow in a blizzard and all but obliterated the landscape. The Navajo came out of his house and took possession of Angelica by her bridle-bit. At first he did not open his lips, merely stood holding Father Latour's very fine white hand in his very fine dark one, and looked into his face with a message of sorrow and resignation in his deep-set, eagle eyes. A wave of feeling passed over his bronze features as he said slowly:

"My friend has come."

That was all, but it was everything; welcome, confidence, appreciation.

For his lodging the Bishop was given a solitary hogan, a little apart from the settlement. Eusabio quickly furnished it with his best skins and blankets, and told his guest that he must tarry a few days there and recover from his fatigue. His mules were tired, the Indian said, the Padre himself looked weary, and the way to Santa Fé was long.

The Bishop thanked him and said he would stay three days; that he had need for reflection. His mind had been taken up with practical matters ever since he left home. This seemed a spot where a man might get his thoughts together. The river, a considerable stream at this time of the year, wound among mounds and dunes of loose sand which whirled through the air all day in the boisterous spring winds. The sand banked up against the hogan the Bishop occupied, and filtered through chinks in the walls, which were made of saplings plastered with clay.

Beside the river was a grove of tall, naked cottonwoods—trees of great antiquity and enormous size—so large that they seemed to belong to a bygone age. They grew far apart, and their strange twisted shapes must have come about from the ceaseless winds that bent them to the east and scoured them with sand, and from the fact that they lived with very little water,—the river was nearly dry here for most of the year. The trees rose out of the ground at a slant, and forty or fifty feet above the earth all these white, dry trunks changed their direction, grew back over their base line. Some split into great forks which arched down almost to the ground; some did not fork at all, but the main trunk dipped downward in a strong curve, as if drawn by a bow-string; and some terminated in a thick coruscation of growth, like a crooked palm tree. They were all living trees, yet they seemed to be of old, dead, dry wood, and had very scant foliage. High up in the forks, or at the end of a preposterous length of twisted bough, would burst a faint bouquet of delicate green leaves—out of all keeping with the great lengths of seasoned white trunk and branches. The grove looked like a winter wood of giant trees, with clusters of mistletoe growing among the bare boughs.

Navajo hospitality is not intrusive. Eusabio made the Bishop understand that he was glad to have him there, and let him alone. Father Latour lived for three days in an almost perpetual sand-storm—cut off from even this remote little Indian camp by moving walls and tapestries of sand. He either sat in his house and listened to the wind, or walked abroad under those aged, wind-distorted trees, muffled in an Indian blanket, which he kept drawn up over his mouth and nose. Since his arrival he had undertaken to decide whether he would be justified in recalling Father Vaillant from Tucson. The Vicar's occasional letters, brought by travellers, showed that he was highly content where he was, restoring the old mission church of St. Xavier del Bac, which he declared to be the most beautiful church on the continent, though it had been neglected for more than two hundred years.

Since Father Vaillant went away the Bishop's burdens had grown heavier and heavier. The new priests from Auvergne were all good men, faithful and untiring in carrying out his wishes; but they were still strangers to the country, timid about making decisions, and referred every difficulty to their Bishop. Father Latour needed his Vicar, who had so much tact with the natives, so much sympathy with all their short-comings. When they were together, he was always curbing Father Vaillant's hopeful rashness—but left alone, he greatly missed that very quality. And he missed Father Vaillant's companionship—why not admit it?

Although Jean Marie Latour and Joseph Vaillant were born in neighbouring parishes in the Puy-de-Dôme, as children they had not known each other. The Latours were an old family of scholars and professional men, while the Vaillants were people of a much humbler station in the provincial world. Besides, little Joseph had been away from home much of the time, up on the farm in the Volvic mountains with his grandfather, where the air was especially pure, and the country quiet salutary for a child of nervous temperament. The two boys had not come together until they were Seminarians at Montferrand, in Clermont.

When Jean Marie was in his second year at the Seminary, he was standing on the recreation ground one day at the opening of the term, looking with curiosity at the new students. In the group, he noticed one of peculiarly unpromising appearance; a boy of nineteen who was undersized, very pale, homely in feature, with a wart on his chin and tow-coloured hair that made him look like a German. This boy seemed to feel his glance, and came up at once, as if he had been called. He was apparently quite unconscious of his homeliness, was not at all shy, but intensely interested in his new surroundings. He asked Jean Latour his name, where he came from, and his father's occupation. Then he said with great simplicity:

"My father is a baker, the best in Riom. In fact, he's a remarkable baker."

Young Latour was amused, but expressed polite appreciation of this confidence. The queer lad went on to tell him about his brother and his aunt, and his clever little sister, Philomène. He asked how long Latour had been at the Seminary.

"Have you always intended to take orders? So have I, but I very nearly went into the army instead."

The year previous, after the surrender of Algiers, there had been a military review at Clermont, a great display of uniforms and military bands, and stirring speeches about the glory of French arms. Young Joseph Vaillant had lost his head in the excitement, and had signed up for a volunteer without consulting his father. He gave Latour a vivid account of his patriotic emotions, of his father's displeasure, and his own subsequent remorse. His mother had wished him to become a priest. She died when he was thirteen, and ever since then he had meant to carry out her wish and to dedicate his life to the service of the Divine Mother. But that one day, among the bands and the uniforms, he had forgotten everything but his desire to serve France.

Suddenly young Vaillant broke off, saying that he must write a letter before the hour was over, and tucking up his gown he ran away at full speed. Latour stood looking after him, resolved that he would take this new boy under his protection. There was something about the baker's son that had given their meeting the colour of an adventure; he meant to repeat it. In that first encounter, he chose the lively, ugly boy for his friend. It was instantaneous. Latour himself was much cooler and more critical in temper; hard to please, and often a little grey in mood.

During their Seminary years he had easily surpassed his friend in scholarship, but he always realized that Joseph excelled him in the fervour of his faith. After they became missionaries, Joseph had learned to speak English, and later, Spanish, more readily than he. To be sure, he spoke both languages very incorrectly at first, but he had no vanity about grammar or refinement of phrase. To communicate with peons, he was quite willing to speak like a peon.

Though the Bishop had worked with Father Joseph for twenty-five years now, he could not reconcile the contradictions of his nature. He simply accepted them, and, when Joseph had been away for a long while, realized that he loved them all. His Vicar was one of the most truly spiritual men he had ever known, though he was so passionately attached to many of the things of this world. Fond as he was of good eating and drinking, he not only rigidly observed all the fasts of the Church, but he never complained about the hardness and scantiness of the fare on his long missionary journeys. Father Joseph's relish for good wine might have been a fault in another man. But always frail in body, he seemed to need some quick physical stimulant to support his sudden flights of purpose and imagination. Time and again the Bishop had seen a good dinner, a bottle of claret, transformed into spiritual energy under his very eyes. From a little feast that would make other men heavy and desirous of repose, Father Vaillant would rise up revived, and work for ten or twelve hours with that ardour and thoroughness which accomplished such lasting results.

The Bishop had often been embarrassed by his Vicar's persistence in begging for the parish, for the Cathedral fund and the distant missions. Yet for himself, Father Joseph was scarcely acquisitive to the point of decency. He owned nothing in the world but his mule, Contento. Though he received rich vestments from his sister in Riom, his daily apparel was rough and shabby. The Bishop had a large and valuable library, at least, and many comforts for his house. There were his beautiful skins and blankets—presents from Eusabio and his other Indian friends. The Mexican women, skilled in needlework and lace-making and hem-stitching, presented him with fine linen for his person, his bed, and his table. He had silver plate, given him by the Olivares and others of his rich parishioners. But Father Vaillant was like the saints of the early Church, literally without personal possessions.

In his youth, Joseph had wished to lead a life of seclusion and solitary devotion; but the truth was, he could not be happy for long without human intercourse. And he liked almost everyone. In Ohio, when they used to travel together in stage-coaches, Father Latour had noticed that every time a new passenger pushed his way into the already crowded stage, Joseph would look pleased and interested, as if this were an agreeable addition—whereas he himself felt annoyed, even if he concealed it. The ugly conditions of life in Ohio had never troubled Joseph. The hideous houses and churches, the ill-kept farms and gardens, the slovenly, sordid aspect of the towns and countryside, which continually depressed Father Latour, he seemed scarcely to perceive. One would have said he had no feeling for comeliness or grace. Yet music was a passion with him. In Sandusky it had been his delight to spend evening after evening with his German choir-master, training the young people to sing Bach oratorios.

Nothing one could say of Father Vaillant explained him. The man was much greater than the sum of his qualities. He added a glow to whatever kind of human society he was dropped down into. A Navajo hogan, some abjectly poor little huddle of Mexican huts, or a company of Monsignori and Cardinals at Rome—it was all the same.

The last time the Bishop was in Rome he had heard an amusing story from Monsignor Mazzucchi, who had been secretary to Gregory XVI at the time when Father Vaillant went from his Ohio mission for his first visit to the Holy City.

Joseph had stayed in Rome for three months, living on about forty cents a day and leaving nothing unseen. He several times asked Mazzucchi to secure him a private audience with the Pope. The secretary liked the missionary from Ohio; there was something abrupt and lively and naïf about him, a kind of freshness he did not often find in the priests who flocked to Rome. So he arranged an interview at which only the Holy Father and Father Vaillant and Mazzucchi were present.

The missionary came in, attended by a chamberlain who carried two great black valises full of objects to be blessed—instead of one, as was customary. After his reception, Father Joseph began to pour out such a vivid account of his missions and brother missionaries, that both the Holy Father and the secretary forgot to take account of time, and the audience lasted three times as long as such interviews were supposed to last. Gregory XVI, that aristocratic and autocratic prelate, who stood so consistently on the wrong side in European politics, and was the enemy of Free Italy, had done more than any of his predecessors to propagate the Faith in remote parts of the world. And here was a missionary after his own heart. Father Vaillant asked for blessings for himself, his fellow priests, his missions, his Bishop. He opened his big valises like pedlars' packs, full of crosses, rosaries, prayer-books, medals, breviaries, on which he begged more than the usual blessing. The astonished chamberlain had come and gone several times, and Mazzucchi at last reminded the Holy Father that he had other engagements. Father Vaillant caught up his two valises himself, the chamberlain not being there at the moment, and thus laden, was bowing himself backward out of the presence, when the Pope rose from his chair and lifted his hand, not in benediction but in salutation, and called out to the departing missionary, as one man to another, "*Coraggio, Americano!*"

Bishop Latour found his Navajo house favourable for reflection, for recalling the past and planning the future. He wrote long letters to his brother and to old friends in France. The hogan was isolated like a ship's cabin on the ocean, with the murmuring of great winds about it. There was no opening except the door, always open, and the air without had the turbid yellow light of sand-storms. All day long the sand came in through the cracks in the walls and formed little ridges on the earth floor. It rattled like sleet upon the dead leaves of the tree-branch roof. This house was so frail a shelter that one seemed to be sitting in the heart of a world made of dusty earth and moving air.

4
Eusabio

On the third day of his visit with Eusabio, the Bishop wrote a somewhat formal letter of recall to his Vicar, and then went for his daily walk in the desert. He stayed out until sunset, when the wind fell and the air cleared to a crystal sharpness. As he was returning, still a mile or more up the river, he heard the deep sound of a cottonwood drum, beaten softly. He surmised that the sound came from Eusabio's house, and that his friend was at home.

Retracing his steps to the settlement, Father Latour found Eusabio seated beside his doorway, singing in the Navajo language and beating softly on one end of his long drum. Before him two very little Indian boys, about four and five years old, were dancing to the music, on the hard beaten ground. Two women, Eusabio's wife and sister, looked on from the deep twilight of the hut.

The little boys did not notice the stranger's approach. They were entirely engrossed in their occupation, their faces serious, their chocolate-coloured eyes half closed. The Bishop stood watching the flowing, supple movements of their arms and shoulders, the sure rhythm of their tiny moccasined feet, no larger than cottonwood leaves, as without a word of instruction they followed the irregular and strangely-accented music. Eusabio himself wore an expression of religious gravity. He sat with the drum between his knees, his broad shoulders bent forward; a crimson *banda* covered his forehead to hold his black hair. The silver on his dark wrists glittered as he stroked the drumhead with a stick or merely tapped it with his fingers. When he finished the song he was singing, he rose and introduced the little boys, his nephews, by their Indian names, Eagle Feather and Medicine Mountain, after which he nodded to them in dismissal. They vanished into the house. Eusabio handed the drum to his wife and walked away with his guest.

"Eusabio," said the Bishop, "I want to send a letter to Father Vaillant, at Tucson. I will send Jacinto with it, provided you can spare me one of your people to accompany me back to Santa Fé."

"I myself will ride with you to the Villa," said Eusabio. The Navajos still called the capital by its old name.

Accordingly, on the following morning, Jacinto was dispatched southward, and Father Latour and Eusabio, with their pack-mule, rode to the east.

The ride back to Santa Fé was something under four hundred miles. The weather alternated between blinding sand-storms and brilliant sunlight. The sky was as full of motion and change as the desert beneath it was monotonous and still,—and there was so much sky, more than at sea, more than anywhere else in the world. The plain was there, under one's feet, but what one saw when one looked about was that brilliant blue world of stinging air and moving cloud. Even the mountains were mere ant-hills under it. Elsewhere the sky is the roof of the world; but here the earth was the floor of the sky. The landscape one longed for when one was far away, the thing all about one, the world one actually lived in, was the sky, the sky!

Travelling with Eusabio was like travelling with the landscape made human. He accepted chance and weather as the country did, with a sort of grave enjoyment. He talked little, ate little, slept anywhere, preserved a countenance open and warm, and like Jacinto he had unfailing good manners. The Bishop was rather surprised that he stopped so often by the way to gather flowers. One morning he came back with the mules, holding a bunch of crimson flowers—long, tube-shaped bells, that hung lightly from one side of a naked stem and trembled in the wind.

"The Indians call rainbow flower," he said, holding them up and making the red tubes quiver. "It is early for these."

When they left the rock or tree or sand dune that had sheltered them for the night, the Navajo was careful to obliterate every trace of their temporary occupation. He buried the embers of the fire and the remnants of food, unpiled any stones he had piled together, filled up the holes he had scooped in the sand. Since this was exactly Jacinto's procedure, Father Latour judged that, just as it was the white man's way to assert himself in any landscape, to change it, make it over a little (at least to leave some mark of memorial of his sojourn), it was the Indian's way to pass through a country without disturbing anything; to pass and leave no trace, like fish through the water, or birds through the air.

It was the Indian manner to vanish into the landscape, not to stand out against it. The Hopi villages that were set upon rock mesas were made to look like the rock on which they sat, were imperceptible at a distance. The Navajo hogans, among the sand and willows, were made of sand and willows. None of the pueblos would at that time admit glass windows into their dwellings. The reflection of the sun on the glazing was to them ugly and unnatural—even dangerous. Moreover, these Indians disliked novelty and change. They came and went by the old paths worn into the rock by the feet of their fathers, used the old natural stairway of stone to climb to their mesa towns, carried water from the old springs, even after white men had dug wells.

In the working of silver or drilling of turquoise the Indians had exhaustless patience; upon their blankets and belts and ceremonial robes they lavished their skill and pains. But their conception of decoration did not extend to the landscape. They seemed to have none of the European's desire to "master" nature, to arrange and re-create. They spent their ingenuity in the other direction; in accommodating themselves to the scene in which they found themselves. This was not so much from indolence, the Bishop thought, as from an inherited caution and respect. It was as if the great country were asleep, and they wished to carry on their lives without awakening it; or as if the spirits of earth and air and water were things not to antagonize and arouse. When they hunted, it was with the same discretion; an Indian hunt was never a slaughter. They ravaged neither the rivers nor the forest, and if they irrigated, they took as little water as would serve their needs. The land and all that it bore they treated with consideration; not attempting to improve it, they never desecrated it.

As Father Latour and Eusabio approached Albuquerque, they occasionally fell in with company; Indians going to and fro on the long winding trails across the plain, or up into the Sandia mountains. They had all of them the same quiet way of moving, whether their pace was swift or slow, and the same unobtrusive demeanour: an Indian wrapped in his bright blanket, seated upon his mule or walking beside it, moving through the pale new-budding sagebrush, winding among the sand waves, as if it were his business to pass unseen and unheard through a country awakening with spring.

North of Laguna two Zuñi runners sped by them, going somewhere east on "Indian business." They saluted Eusabio by gestures with the open palm, but did not stop. They coursed over the sand with the fleetness of young antelope, their bodies disappearing and reappearing among the sand dunes, like the shadows that eagles cast in their strong, unhurried flight.

BOOK EIGHT

Gold Under Pike's Peak

1
Cathedral

Father Vaillant had been in Santa Fé nearly three weeks, and as yet nothing had been revealed to him that warranted his Bishop in calling him back from Tucson. One morning Fructosa came into the garden to tell him that lunch would be earlier than usual, as the Bishop was going to ride somewhere that afternoon. Half an hour later he joined his superior in the dining-room.

The Bishop lunched alone. That was the hour when he could most conveniently entertain a priest from one of the distant parishes, an army officer, an American trader, a visitor from Old Mexico or California. He had no parlour—his dining room served that purpose. It was long and cool, with windows only at the west end, opening into the garden. The green jalousies let in a tempered light. Sunbeams played on the white, rounded walls and twinkled on the glass and silver of the sideboard. When Madame Olivares left Santa Fé to return to New Orleans and sold her effects at auction, Father Latour bought her sideboard, and the dining-table around which friends had so often gathered. Doña Isabella gave him her silver coffee service and candelabra for remembrance. They were the only ornaments of the severe and shadowy room.

The Bishop was already at his place when Father Joseph entered. "Fructosa has told you why we are lunching early? We will take a ride this afternoon. I have something to show you."

"Very good. Perhaps you have noticed that I am a little restless. I don't know when I have been two weeks out of the saddle before. When I go to visit Contento in his stall, he looks at me reprovingly. He will grow too fat."

The Bishop smiled, with a shade of sarcasm on his upper lip. He knew his Joseph. "Ah, well," he said carelessly, "a little rest will not hurt him, after coming six hundred miles from Tucson. You can take him out this afternoon, and I will ride Angelica."

The two priests left Santa Fé a little after midday, riding west. The Bishop did not disclose his objective, and the Vicar asked no questions. Soon they left the wagon road and took a trail running straight south, through an empty greasewood country sloping gradually in the direction of the naked blue Sandia mountains.

At about four o'clock they came out upon a ridge high over the Rio Grande valley. The trail dropped down a long decline at this point and wound about the foot of the Sandias into Albuquerque, some sixty miles away.

This ridge was covered with cone-shaped, rocky hills, thinly clad with piñons, and the rock was a curious shade of green, something between sea-green and olive. The thin, pebbly earth, which was merely the rock pulverized by weather, had the same green tint. Father Latour rode to an isolated hill that beetled over the western edge of the ridge, just where the trail descended. This hill stood up high and quite alone, boldly facing the declining sun and the blue Sandias. As they drew close to it, Father Vaillant noticed that on the western face the earth had been scooped away, exposing a rugged wall of rock—not green like the surrounding hills, but yellow, a strong golden ochre, very much like the gold of the sunlight that was now beating upon it. Picks and crowbars lay about, and fragments of stone, freshly broken off.

"It is curious, is it not, to find one yellow hill among all these green ones?" remarked the Bishop, stooping to pick up a piece of the stone. "I have ridden over these hills in every direction, but this is the only one of its kind." He stood regarding the chip of yellow rock that lay in his palm. As he had a very special way of handling objects that were sacred, he extended that manner to things which he considered beautiful. After a moment of silence he looked up at the rugged wall, gleaming gold above them. "That hill, *Blanchet*, is my Cathedral."

Father Joseph looked at his Bishop, then at the cliff, blinking. "*Vraiment?* Is the stone hard enough? A good colour, certainly; something like the colonnade of St. Peter's."

The Bishop smoothed the piece of rock with his thumb. "It is more like something nearer home—I mean, nearer Clermont. When I look up at this rock I can almost feel the Rhone behind me."

"Ah, you mean the old Palace of the Popes, at Avignon! Yes, you are right, it is very like. At this hour, it is like this."

The Bishop sat down on a boulder, still looking up at the cliff. "It is the stone I have always wanted, and I found it quite by chance. I was coming back from Isleta. I had been to see old Padre Jesus when he was dying. I had never come by this trail, but when I reached Santo Domingo I found the road so washed by a heavy rain that I turned out and decided to try this way home. I rode up here from the west in the late afternoon; this hill confronted me as it confronts us now, and I knew instantly that it was my Cathedral."

"Oh, such things are never accidents, Jean. But it will be a long while before you can think of building."

"Not so very long, I hope. I should like to complete it before I die—if God so wills. I wish to leave nothing to chance, or to the mercy of American builders. I had rather keep the old adobe church we have now than help to build one of those horrible structures they are putting up in the Ohio cities. I want a plain church, but I want a good one. I shall certainly never lift my hand to build a clumsy affair of red brick, like an English coach-house. Our own Midi Romanesque is the right style for this country."

Father Vaillant sniffed and wiped his glasses. "If you once begin thinking about architects and styles, Jean! And if you don't get American builders, whom will you get, pray?"

"I have an old friend in Toulouse who is a very fine architect. I talked this matter over with him when I was last at home. He cannot come himself; he is afraid of the long sea voyage, and not used to horseback travel. But he has a young son, still at his studies, who is eager to undertake the work. Indeed, his father writes me that it has become the young man's dearest ambition to build the first Romanesque church in the New World. He will have studied the right models; he thinks our old churches of the Midi the most beautiful in France. When we are ready, he will come and bring with him a couple of good French stone-cutters. They will certainly be no more expensive than workmen from St. Louis. Now that I have found exactly the stone I want, my Cathedral seems to me already begun. This hill is only about fifteen miles from Santa Fé; there is an upgrade, but it is gradual. Hauling the stone will be easier than I could have hoped for."

"You plan far ahead." Father Vaillant looked at his friend wonderingly. "Well, that is what a Bishop should be able to do. As for me, I see only what is under my nose. But I had no idea you were going in for fine building, when everything about us is so poor—and we ourselves are so poor."

"But the Cathedral is not for us, Father Joseph. We build for the future—better not lay a stone unless we can do that. It would be a shame to any man coming from a Seminary that is one of the architectural treasures of France, to make another ugly church on this continent where there are so many already."

"You are probably right. I had never thought of it before. It never occurred to me that we could have anything but an Ohio church here. Your ancestors helped to build Clermont Cathedral, I remember; two building Bishops de la Tour back in the thirteenth century. Time brings things to pass, certainly. I had no idea you were taking all this so much to heart."

Father Latour laughed. "Is a cathedral a thing to be taken lightly, after all?"

"Oh, no, certainly not!" Father Vaillant moved his shoulders uneasily. He did not himself know why he hung back in this.

The base of the hill before which they stood was already in shadow, subdued to the tone of rich yellow clay, but the top was still melted gold—a colour that throbbed in the last rays of the sun. The Bishop turned away at last with a sigh of deep content. "Yes," he said slowly, "that rock will do very well. And now we must be starting home. Every time I come here, I like this stone better. I could hardly have hoped that God would gratify my personal taste, my vanity, if you will, in this way. I tell you, *Blanchet*, I would rather have found that hill of yellow rock than have come into a fortune to spend in charity. The Cathedral is near my heart, for many reasons. I hope you do not think me very worldly."

As they rode home through the sage-brush silvered by moonlight, Father Vaillant was still wondering why he had been called home from saving souls in Arizona, and wondering why a poor missionary Bishop should care so much about a building. He himself was eager to have the Cathedral begun; but whether it was Midi Romanesque or Ohio German in style, seemed to him of little consequence.

2
A Letter from Leavenworth

The day after the Bishop and his Vicar rode to the yellow rock the weekly post arrived at Santa Fé. It brought the Bishop many letters, and he was shut in his study all morning. At lunch hour he told Father Vaillant that he would require his company that evening to consider with him a letter of great importance from the Bishop of Leavenworth.

This letter of many pages was concerned with events that were happening in Colorado, in a part of the Rocky Mountains very little known. Though it was only a few hundred miles north of Santa Fé, communication with that region was so infrequent that news travelled to Santa Fé from Europe more quickly than from Pike's Peak. Under the shadow of that peak rich gold deposits had been discovered within the last year, but Father Vaillant had first heard of this through a letter from France. Word of it had reached the Atlantic coast, crossed to Europe, and come from there back to the Southwest, more quickly than it could filter down through the few hundred miles of unexplored mountains and gorges between Cherry Creek and Santa Fé. While Father Vaillant was at Tucson he had received a letter from his brother Marius, in Auvergne, and was vexed that so much of it was taken up with inquiries about the gold rush to Colorado, of which he had never heard, while Marius gave him but little news of the war in Italy, which seemed relatively near and much more important.

That congested heaping up of the Rocky Mountain chain about Pike's Peak was a blank space on the continent at this time. Even the fur trappers, coming down from Wyoming to Taos with their pelts, avoided that humped granite backbone. Only a few years before, Frémont had tried to penetrate the Colorado Rockies, and his party had come half-starved into Taos at last, having eaten most of their mules. But within twelve months everything had changed. Wandering prospectors had found large deposits of gold along Cherry Creek, and the mountains that were solitary a year ago were now full of people. Wagon trains were streaming westward across the prairies from the Missouri River.

The Bishop of Leavenworth wrote Father Latour that he himself had just returned from a visit to Colorado. He had found the slopes under Pike's Peak dotted with camps, the gorges black with placer miners; thousands of people were living in tents and shacks, Denver City was full of saloons and gambling-rooms; and among all the wanderers and wastrels were many honest men, hundreds of good Catholics, and not one priest. The young men were adrift in a lawless society without spiritual guidance. The old men died from exposure and mountain pneumonia, with no one to give them the last rites of the Church.

This new and populous community must, for the present, the Kansas Bishop wrote, be accounted under Father Latour's jurisdiction. His great diocese, already enlarged by thousands of square miles to the south and west, must now, on the north, take in the still undefined but suddenly important region of the Colorado Rockies. The Bishop of Leavenworth begged him to send a priest there as soon as possible,—an able one, by all means, not only devoted, but resourceful and intelligent, one who would be at his ease with all sorts of men. He must take his bedding and camp outfit, medicines and provisions, and clothing for the severe winter. At Camp Denver there was nothing to be bought but tobacco and whisky. There were no women there, and no cook stoves. The miners lived on half-baked dough and alcohol. They did not even keep the mountain water pure, and so died of fever. All the living conditions were abominable.

In the evening, after dinner, Father Latour read this letter aloud to Father Vaillant in his study. When he had finished, he put down the closely written pages.

"You have been complaining of inactivity, Father Joseph; here is your opportunity."

Father Joseph, who had been growing more and more restless during the reading of the letter, said merely: "So now I must begin speaking English again! I can start tomorrow if you wish it."

The Bishop shook his head. "Not so fast. There will be no hospitable Mexicans to receive you at the end of this journey. You must take your living with you. We will have a wagon built for you, and choose your outfit carefully. Tranquilino's brother, Sabino, will be your driver. This, I fear, will be the hardest mission you have ever undertaken."

The two priests talked until a late hour. There was Arizona to be considered; somebody must be found to continue Father Vaillant's work there. Of all the countries he knew, that desert and its yellow people were the dearest to him. But it was the discipline of his life to break ties; to say farewell and move on into the unknown.

Before he went to bed that night Father Joseph greased his boots and trimmed the calloused spots on his feet with an old razor. At the Mexican village of Chimayo, over toward the Truchas mountains, the good people were especially devoted to a little equestrian image of Santiago in their church, and they made him a new pair of boots every few months, insisting that he went abroad at night and wore out his shoes, even on horseback. When Father Joseph stayed there, he used to tell them he wished that, in addition to the consecration of the hands, God had provided some special blessing for the missionary's feet.

He recalled affectionately an incident which concerned this Santiago of Chimayo. Some years ago Father Joseph was asked to go to the *calabozo* at Santa Fé to see a murderer from Chimayo. The prisoner proved to be a boy of twenty, very gentle in face and manner. His name was Ramón Armajillo. He had been passionately fond of cock-fighting, and it was his undoing. He had bred a rooster that never lost a battle, but had slit the necks of cocks in all the little towns about. At last Ramón brought the bird to Santa Fé to match him with a famous cock there, and half a dozen Chimayo boys came along and put up everything they had on Ramón's rooster. The betting was heavy on both sides, and the gate receipts also were to go to the winner. After a somewhat doubtful beginning, Ramón's cock neatly ripped the jugular vein of his opponent; but the owner of the defeated bird, before anyone could stop him, reached into the ring and wrung the victor's neck. Before he had dropped the limp bunch of feathers from his hand, Ramón's knife was in his heart. It all happened in a flash—some of the witnesses even insisted that the death of the man and the death of the cock were simultaneous. All agreed that there was not time for a man to catch his breath between the whirl of the wrist and the gleam of the knife. Unfortunately the American judge was a very stupid man, who disliked Mexicans and hoped to wipe out cock-fighting. He accepted as evidence statements made by the murdered man's friends to the effect that Ramón had repeatedly threatened his life.

When Father Vaillant went to see the boy in his cell a few days before his execution, he found him making a pair of tiny buckskin boots, as if for a doll, and Ramón told him they were for the little Santiago in the church at home. His family would come up to Santa Fé for the hanging, and they would take the boots back to Chimayo, and perhaps the little saint would say a good word for him.

Rubbing oil into his boots by candlelight, Father Vaillant sighed. The criminals with whom he would have to do in Colorado would hardly be of that type, he told himself.

3
Auspice Maria!

The construction of Father Vaillant's wagon took a month. It must be a wagon of very unusual design, capable of carrying a great deal, yet light enough and narrow enough to wind through the mountain gorges beyond Pueblo,—where there were no roads at all except the rocky ravines cut out by streams that flowed full in the spring but would be dry now in the autumn. While his wagon was building, Father Joseph was carefully selecting his stores, and the furnishings for a small chapel which he meant to construct of saplings or canvas immediately upon his arrival at Camp Denver. Moreover, there were his valises full of medals, crosses, rosaries, coloured pictures and religious pamphlets. For himself, he required no books but his breviary.

In the Bishop's court-yard he sorted and re-sorted his cargo, always finding a more necessary article for which a less necessary had to be discarded. Fructosa and Magdalena were frequently called upon to help him, and when a box was finally closed, Fructosa had it put away in the wood-shed. She had noticed the Bishop's brows contract slightly when he came upon these trunks and chests in his hallway and dining-room. All the bedding and clothing was packed in great sacks of dressed calfskin, which Sabino procured from old Mexican settlers. These were already going out of fashion, but in the early days they were the poor man's trunk.

Bishop Latour also was very busy at this time, training a new priest from Clermont; riding about with him among the distant parishes and trying to give him an understanding of the people. As a Bishop, he could only approve Father Vaillant's eagerness to be gone, and the enthusiasm with which he turned to hardships of a new kind. But as a man, he was a little hurt that his old comrade should leave him without one regret. He seemed to know, as if it had been revealed to him, that this was a final break; that their lives would part here, and that they would never work together again. The bustle of preparation in his own house was painful to him, and he was glad to be abroad among the parishes.

One day when the Bishop had just returned from Albuquerque, Father Vaillant came in to luncheon in high spirits. He had been out for a drive in his new wagon, and declared that it was satisfactory at last. Sabino was ready, and he thought they would start the day after to-morrow. He diagrammed his route on the table-cloth, and went over the catalogue of his equipment. The Bishop was tired and scarcely touched his food, but Father Joseph ate generously, as he was apt to do when fired by a new project.

After Fructosa had brought the coffee, he leaned back in his chair and turned to his friend with a beaming face. "I often think, Jean, how you were an unconscious agent in the hands of Providence when you recalled me from Tucson. I seemed to be doing the most important work of my life there, and you recalled me for no reason at all, apparently. You did not know why, and I did not know why. We were both acting in the dark. But Heaven knew what was happening on Cherry Creek, and moved us like chessmen on the board. When the call came, I was here to answer it—by a miracle, indeed."

Father Latour put down his silver coffee-cup. "Miracles are all very well, Joseph, but I see none here. I sent for you because I felt the need of your companionship. I used my authority as a Bishop to gratify my personal wish. That was selfish, if you will, but surely natural enough. We are countrymen, and are bound by early memories. And that two friends, having come together, should part and go their separate ways—that is natural, too. No, I don't think we need any miracle to explain all this."

Father Vaillant had been wholly absorbed in his preparations for saving souls in the gold camps—blind to everything else. Now it came over him in a flash, how the Bishop had held himself aloof from his activities; it was a very hard thing for Father Latour to let him go; the loneliness of his position had begun to weigh upon him.

Yes, he reflected, as he went quietly to his own room, there was a great difference in their natures. Wherever he went, he soon made friends that took the place of country and family. But Jean, who was at ease in any society and always the flower of courtesy, could not form new ties. It had always been so. He was like that even as a boy; gracious to everyone, but known to a very few. To man's wisdom it would have seemed that a priest with Father Latour's exceptional qualities would have been better placed in some part of the world where scholarship, a handsome person, and delicate perceptions all have their effect; and that a man of much rougher type would have served God well enough as the first Bishop of New Mexico. Doubtless Bishop Latour's successors would be men of a different fibre. But God had his reasons, Father Joseph devoutly believed. Perhaps it pleased Him to grace the beginning of a new era and a vast new diocese by a fine personality. And perhaps, after all, something would remain through the years to come; some ideal, or memory, or legend.

The next afternoon, his wagon loaded and standing ready in the court-yard, Father Vaillant was seated at the Bishop's desk, writing letters to France; a short one to Marius, a long one to his beloved Philomène, telling her of his plunge into the unknown and begging her prayers for his success in the world of gold-crazed men. He wrote rapidly and jerkily, moving his lips as well as his fingers. When the Bishop entered the study, he rose and stood holding the written pages in his hand.

"I did not mean to interrupt you, Joseph, but do you intend to take Contento with you to Colorado?"

Father Joseph blinked. "Why, certainly. I had intended to ride him. However, if you have need for him here—"

"Oh, no. Not at all. But if you take Contento, I will ask you to take Angelica as well. They have a great affection for each other; why separate them indefinitely? One could not explain to them. They have worked long together."

Father Vaillant made no reply. He stood looking intently at the pages of his letter. The Bishop saw a drop of water splash down upon the violet script and spread. He turned quickly and went out through the arched doorway.

At sunrise next morning Father Vaillant set out, Savino driving the wagon, his oldest boy riding Angelica, and Father Joseph himself riding Contento. They took the old road to the northeast, through the sharp red sand-hills spotted with juniper, and the Bishop accompanied them as far as the loop where the road wound out on the top of one of those conical hills, giving the departing traveller his last glimpse of Santa Fé. There Father Joseph drew rein and looked back at the town lying rosy in the morning light, the mountain behind it, and the hills close about it like two encircling arms.

"*Auspice, Maria!*" he murmured as he turned his back on these familiar things.

The Bishop rode home to his solitude. He was forty-seven years old, and he had been a missionary in the New World for twenty years—ten of them in New Mexico. If he were a parish priest at home, there would be nephews coming to him for help in their Latin or a bit of pocket-money; nieces to run into his garden and bring their sewing and keep an eye on his housekeeping. All the way home he indulged in such reflections as any bachelor nearing fifty might have.

But when he entered his study, he seemed to come back to reality, to the sense of a Presence awaiting him. The curtain of the arched doorway had scarcely fallen behind him when that feeling of personal loneliness was gone, and a sense of loss was replaced by a sense of restoration. He sat down before his desk, deep in reflection. It was just this solitariness of love in which a priest's life could be like his Master's. It was not a solitude of atrophy, of negation, but of perpetual flowering. A life need not be cold, or devoid of grace in the worldly sense, if it were filled by Her who was all the graces; Virgin-daughter, Virgin-mother, girl of the people and Queen of Heaven: *le rêve suprême de la chair*. The nursery tale could not vie with Her in simplicity, the wisest theologians could not match Her in profundity.

Here in his own church in Santa Fé there was one of these nursery Virgins, a little wooden figure, very old and very dear to the people. De Vargas, when he recaptured the city for Spain two hundred years ago, had vowed a yearly procession in her honour, and it was still one of the most solemn events of the Christian year in Santa Fé. She was a little wooden figure, about three feet high, very stately in bearing, with a beautiful though rather severe Spanish face. She had a rich wardrobe; a chest full of robes and laces, and gold and silver diadems. The women loved to sew for her and the silversmiths to make her chains and brooches. Father Latour had delighted her wardrobe keepers when he told them he did not believe the Queen of England or the Empress of France had so many costumes. She was their doll and their queen, something to fondle and something to adore, as Mary's Son must have been to Her.

These poor Mexicans, he reflected, were not the first to pour out their love in this simple fashion. Raphael and Titian had made costumes for Her in their time, and the great masters had made music for Her, and the great architects had built cathedrals for Her. Long before Her years on earth, in the long twilight between the Fall and the Redemption, the pagan sculptors were always trying to achieve the image of a goddess who should yet be a woman.

Bishop Latour's premonition was right: Father Vaillant never returned to share his work in New Mexico. Come back he did, to visit his old friends, whenever his busy life permitted. But his destiny was fulfilled in the cold, steely Colorado Rockies, which he never loved as he did the blue mountains of the South. He came back to Santa Fé to recuperate from the illnesses and accidents which consistently punctuated his way; came with the Papal Emissary when Bishop Latour was made Archbishop; but his working life was spent among bleak mountains and comfortless mining camps, looking after lost sheep.

Creede, Durango, Silver City, Central City, over the Continental Divide into Utah,—his strange Episcopal carriage was known throughout that rugged granite world.

It was a covered carriage, on springs, and long enough for him to lie down in at night,—Father Joseph was a very short man. At the back was a luggage box, which could be made into an altar when he celebrated Mass in the open, under a pine tree. He used to say that the mountain torrents were the first road builders, and that wherever they found a way, he could find one. He wore out driver after driver, and his coach was repaired so often and so extensively that long before he abandoned it there was none of the original structure left.

Broken tongues and singletrees, smashed wheels and splintered axles he considered trifling matters. Twice the old carriage itself slipped off the mountain road and rolled down the gorge, with the priest inside. From the first accident of this kind, Father Vaillant escaped with nothing worse than a sprain, and he wrote Bishop Latour that he attributed his preservation to the Archangel Raphael, whose office he had said with unusual fervor that morning. The second time he rolled down a ravine, near Central City, his thigh-bone was broken just below the joint. It knitted in time, but he was lamed for life, and could never ride horseback again.

Before this accident befell him, however, he had one long visit among his friends in Santa Fé and Albuquerque, a renewal of old ties that was like an Indian summer in his life. When he left Denver, he told his congregation there that he was going to the Mexicans to beg for money. The church in Denver was under a roof, but the windows had been boarded up for months because nobody would buy glass for them. In his Denver congregation there were men who owned mines and saw-mills and flourishing businesses, but they needed all their money to push these enterprises. Down among the Mexicans, who owned nothing but a mud house and a burro, he could always raise money. If they had anything at all, they gave.

He called this trip frankly a begging expedition, and he went in his carriage to bring back whatever he could gather. When he got as far as Taos, his Irish driver mutinied. Not another mile over these roads, he said. He knew his own territory, but here he refused to risk his neck and the Padre's. There was then no wagon road from Taos to Santa Fé. It was nearly a fortnight before Father Vaillant found a man who would undertake to get him through the mountains. At last an old driver, schooled on the wagon trains, volunteered; and with the help of ax and pick and shovel, he brought the Episcopal carriage safely to Santa Fé and into the Bishop's court-yard.

Once again among his own people, as he still called them, Father Joseph opened his campaign, and the poor Mexicans began taking dollars out of their shirts and boots (favourite places for carrying money) to pay for windows in the Denver church. His petitions did not stop with windows—indeed, they only began there. He told the sympathetic women of Santa Fé and Albuquerque about all the stupid, unnecessary discomforts of his life in Denver, discomforts that amounted to improprieties. It was a part of the Wild West attitude to despise the decencies of life. He told them how glad he was to sleep in good Mexican beds once more. In Denver he lay on a mattress stuffed with straw; a French priest who was visiting him had pulled out a long stem of hay that stuck through the thin ticking, and called it an American feather. His dining-table was made of planks covered with oilcloth. He had no linen at all, neither sheets nor serviettes, and he used his worn-out shirts for face towels. The Mexican women could scarcely bear to hear of such things. Nobody in Colorado planted gardens, Father Vaillant related; nobody would stick a shovel into the earth for anything less than gold. There was no butter, no milk, no eggs, no fruit. He lived on dough and cured hog meat.

Within a few weeks after his arrival, six feather-beds were sent to the Bishop's house for Father Vaillant; dozens of linen sheets, embroidered pillow-cases and table-cloths and napkins; strings of chili and boxes of beans and dried fruit. The little settlement of Chimayo sent a roll of their finest blankets.

As these gifts arrived, Father Joseph put them in the woodhouse, knowing well that the Bishop was always embarrassed by his readiness to receive presents. But one morning Father Latour had occasion to go into the woodhouse, and he saw for himself.

"Father Joseph," he remonstrated, "you will never be able to take all these things back to Denver. Why, you would need an ox-cart to carry them!"

"Very well," replied Father Joseph, "then God will send me an ox-cart."

And He did, with a driver to take the cart as far as Pueblo.

On the morning of his departure for home, when his carriage was ready, the cart covered with tarpaulins and the oxen yoked, Father Vaillant, who had been hurrying everyone since the first streak of light, suddenly became deliberate. He went into the Bishop's study and sat down, talking to him of unimportant matters, lingering as if there were something still undone.

"Well, we are getting older, Jean," he said abruptly, after a short silence.

The Bishop smiled. "Ah, yes. We are not young men any more. One of these departures will be the last."

Father Vaillant nodded. "Whenever God wills. I am ready." He rose and began to pace the floor, addressing his friend without looking at him. "But it has not been so bad, Jean? We have done the things we used to plan to do, long ago, when we were Seminarians,—at least some of them. To fulfil the dreams of one's youth; that is the best that can happen to a man. No worldly success can take the place of that."

"*Blanchet*," said the Bishop rising, "you are a better man than I. You have been a great harvester of souls, without pride and without shame—and I am always a little cold—*un pédant*, as you used to say. If hereafter we have stars in our crowns, yours will be a constellation. Give me your blessing."

He knelt, and Father Vaillant, having blessed him, knelt and was blessed in turn. They embraced each other for the past—for the future.

Book Nine

Death Comes for the Archbishop

1

When that devout nun, Mother Superior Philomène, died at a great age in her native Riom, among her papers were found several letters from Archbishop Latour, one dated December 1888, only a few months before his death. "*Since your brother was called to his reward,*" he wrote, "*I feel nearer to him than before. For many years Duty separated us, but death has brought us together. The time is not far distant when I shall join him. Meanwhile, I am enjoying to the full that period of reflection which is the happiest conclusion to a life of action.*"

This period of reflection the Archbishop spent on his little country estate, some four miles north of Santa Fé. Long before his retirement from the cares of the diocese, Father Latour bought those few acres in the red sand-hills near the Tesuque pueblo, and set out an orchard which would be bearing when the time came for him to rest. He chose this place in the red hills spotted with juniper against the advice of his friends, because he believed it to be admirably suited for the growing of fruit.

Once when he was riding out to visit the Tesuque mission, he had followed a stream and come upon this spot, where he found a little Mexican house and a garden shaded by an apricot tree of such great size as he had never seen before. It had two trunks, each of them thicker than a man's body, and though evidently very old, it was full of fruit. The apricots were large, beautifully coloured, and of superb flavour. Since this tree grew against the hill-side, the Archbishop concluded that the exposure there must be excellent for fruit. He surmised that the heat of the sun, reflected from the rocky hill-slope up into the tree, gave the fruit an even temperature, warmth from two sides, such as brings the wall peaches to perfection in France.

The old Mexican who lived there said the tree must be two hundred years old; it had been just like this when his grandfather was a boy, and had always borne luscious apricots like these. The old man would be glad to sell the place and move into Santa Fé, the Bishop found, and he bought it a few weeks later. In the spring he set out his orchard and a few rows of acacia trees. Some years afterward he built a little adobe house, with a chapel, high up on the hill-side overlooking the orchard. Thither he used to go for rest and at seasons of special devotion. After his retirement, he went there to live, though he always kept his study unchanged in the house of the new Archbishop.

In his retirement Father Latour's principal work was the training of the new missionary priests who arrived from France. His successor, the second Archbishop, was also an Auvergnat, from Father Latour's own college, and the clergy of northern New Mexico remained predominantly French. When a company of new priests arrived (they never came singly) Archbishop S—— sent them out to stay with Father Latour for a few months, to receive instruction in Spanish, in the topography of the diocese, in the character and traditions of the different pueblos.

Father Latour's recreation was his garden. He grew such fruit as was hardly to be found even in the old orchards of California: cherries and apricots, apples and quinces, and the peerless pears of France—even the most delicate varieties. He urged the new priests to plant fruit trees wherever they went, and to encourage the Mexicans to add fruit to their starchy diet. Wherever there was a French priest, there should be a garden of fruit trees and vegetables and flowers. He often quoted to his students that passage from their fellow Auvergnat, Pascal: that Man was lost and saved in a garden.

He domesticated and developed the native wild flowers. He had one hill-side solidly clad with that low-growing purple verbena which mats over the hills of New Mexico. It was like a great violet velvet mantle thrown down in the sun; all the shades that the dyers and weavers of Italy and France strove for through centuries, the violet that is full of rose colour and is yet not lavender; the blue that becomes almost pink and then retreats again into sea-dark purple—the true Episcopal colour and countless variations of it.

In the year 1885 there came to New Mexico a young Seminarian, Bernard Ducrot, who became like a son to Father Latour. The story of the old Archbishop's life, often told in the cloisters and class-rooms at Montferrand, had taken hold of this boy's imagination, and he had long waited an opportunity to come. Bernard was handsome in person and of unusual mentality, had in himself the fineness to reverence all that was fine in his venerable Superior. He anticipated Father Latour's every wish, shared his reflections, cherished his reminiscences.

"Surely," the Bishop used to say to the priests, "God himself has sent me this young man to help me through the last years."

2

Throughout the autumn of the year '88 the Bishop was in good health. He had five French priests in his house, and he still rode abroad with them to visit the nearer missions. On Christmas eve, he performed the midnight Mass in the Cathedral at Santa Fé. In January he drove with Bernard to Santa Cruz to see the resident priest, who was ill. While they were on their way home the weather suddenly changed, and a violent rainstorm overtook them. They were in an open buggy and were drenched to the skin before they could reach any Mexican house for shelter.

After arriving home, Father Latour went at once to bed. During the night he slept badly and felt feverish. He called none of his household, but arose at the usual hour before dawn and went into the chapel for his devotions. While he was at prayer, he was seized with a chill. He made his way to the kitchen, and his old cook, Fructosa, alarmed at once, put him to bed and gave him brandy. This chill left him feverish, and he developed a distressing cough.

After keeping quietly to his bed for a few days, the Bishop called young Bernard to him one morning and said:

"Bernard, will you ride into Santa Fé to-day and see the Archbishop for me. Ask him whether it will be quite convenient if I return to occupy my study in his house for a short time. *Je voudrais mourir à Santa Fé.*"

"I will go at once, Father. But you should not be discouraged; one does not die of a cold."

The old man smiled. "I shall not die of a cold, my son. I shall die of having lived."

From that moment on, he spoke only French to those about him, and this sudden relaxing of his rule alarmed his household more than anything else about his condition. When a priest had received bad news from home, or was ill, Father Latour would converse with him in his own language; but at other times he required that all conversation in his house should be in Spanish or English.

Bernard returned that afternoon to say that the Archbishop would be delighted if Father Latour would remain the rest of the winter with him. Magdalena had already begun to air his study and put it in order, and she would be in special attendance upon him during his visit. The Archbishop would send his new carriage to fetch him, as Father Latour had only an open buggy.

"Not to-day, *mon fils*," said the Bishop. "We will choose a day when I am feeling stronger; a fair day, when we can go in my own buggy, and you can drive me. I wish to go late in the afternoon, toward sunset."

Bernard understood. He knew that once, long ago, at that hour of the day, a young Bishop had ridden along the Albuquerque road and seen Santa Fé for the first time. ... And often, when they were driving into town together, the Bishop had paused with Bernard on that hill-top from which Father Vaillant had looked back on Santa Fé, when he went away to Colorado to begin the work that had taken the rest of his life and made him, too, a Bishop in the end.

The old town was better to look at in those days, Father Latour used to tell Bernard with a sigh. In the old days it had an individuality, a style of its own; a tawny adobe town with a few green trees, set in a half-circle of carnelian-coloured hills; that and no more. But the year 1880 had begun a period of incongruous American building. Now, half the plaza square was still adobe, and half was flimsy wooden buildings with double porches, scroll-work and jack-straw posts and banisters painted white. Father Latour said the wooden houses which had so distressed him in Ohio, had followed him. All this was quite wrong for the Cathedral he had been so many years in building,—the Cathedral that had taken Father Vaillant's place in his life after that remarkable man went away.

Father Latour made his last entry into Santa Fé at the end of a brilliant February afternoon; Bernard stopped the horses at the foot of the long street to await the sunset.

Wrapped in his Indian blankets, the old Archbishop sat for a long while, looking at the open, golden face of his Cathedral. How exactly young Molny, his French architect, had done what he wanted! Nothing sensational, simply honest building and good stone-cutting,—good Midi Romanesque of the plainest. And even now, in winter, when the acacia trees before the door were bare, how it was of the South, that church, how it sounded the note of the South!

No one but Molny and the Bishop had ever seemed to enjoy the beautiful site of that building,—perhaps no one ever would. But these two had spent many an hour admiring it. The steep carnelian hills drew up so close behind the church that the individual pine trees thinly wooding their slopes were clearly visible. From the end of the street where the Bishop's buggy stood, the tawny church seemed to start directly out of those rose-coloured hills— with a purpose so strong that it was like action. Seen from this distance, the Cathedral lay against the pine-splashed slopes as against a curtain. When Bernard drove slowly nearer, the backbone of the hills sank gradually, and the towers rose clear into the blue air, while the body of the church still lay against the mountain.

The young architect used to tell the Bishop that only in Italy, or in the opera, did churches leap out of mountains and black pines like that. More than once Molny had called the Bishop from his study to look at the unfinished building when a storm was coming up; then the sky above the mountain grew black, and the carnelian rocks became an intense lavender, all their pine trees strokes of dark purple; the hills drew nearer, the whole background approached like a dark threat.

"Setting," Molny used to tell Father Latour, "is accident. Either a building is a part of a place, or it is not. Once that kinship is there, time will only make it stronger."

The Bishop was recalling this saying of Molny's when a voice out of the present sounded in his ear. It was Bernard.

"A fine sunset, Father. See how red the mountains are growing; Sangre de Cristo."

Yes, Sangre de Cristo; but no matter how scarlet the sunset, those red hills never became vermilion, but a more and more intense rose-carnelian; not the colour of living blood, the Bishop had often reflected, but the colour of the dried blood of saints and martyrs preserved in old churches in Rome, which liquefies upon occasion.

3

The next morning Father Latour wakened with a grateful sense of nearness to his Cathedral—which would also be his tomb. He felt safe under its shadow; like a boat come back to harbour, lying under its own sea-wall. He was in his old study; the Sisters had sent a little iron bed from the school for him, and their finest linen and blankets. He felt a great content at being here, where he had come as a young man and where he had done his work. The room was little changed; the same rugs and skins on the earth floor, the same desk with his candlesticks, the same thick, wavy white walls that muted sound, that shut out the world and gave repose to the spirit.

As the darkness faded into the grey of a winter morning, he listened for the church bells,—and for another sound, that always amused him here; the whistle of a locomotive. Yes, he had come with the buffalo, and he had lived to see railway trains running into Santa Fé. He had accomplished an historic period.

All his relatives at home, and his friends in New Mexico, had expected that the old Archbishop would spend his closing years in France, probably in Clermont, where he could occupy a chair in his old college. That seemed the natural thing to do, and he had given it grave consideration. He had half expected to make some such arrangement the last time he was in Auvergne, just before his retirement from his duties as Archbishop. But in the Old World he found himself homesick for the New. It was a feeling he could not explain; a feeling that old age did not weigh so heavily upon a man in New Mexico as in the Puy-de-Dôme.

He loved the towering peaks of his native mountains, the comeliness of the villages, the cleanness of the country-side, the beautiful lines and cloisters of his own college. Clermont was beautiful,—but he found himself sad there; his heart lay like a stone in his breast. There was too much past, perhaps. . . . When the summer wind stirred the lilacs in the old gardens and shook down the blooms of the horse-chestnuts, he sometimes closed his eyes and thought of the high song the wind was singing in the straight, striped pine trees up in the Navajo forests.

During the day his nostalgia wore off, and by dinnertime it was quite gone. He enjoyed his dinner and his wine, and the company of cultivated men, and usually retired in good spirits. It was in the early morning that he felt the ache in his breast; it had something to do with waking in the early morning. It seemed to him that the grey dawn lasted so long here, the country was a long while in coming to life. The gardens and the fields were damp, heavy mists hung in the valley and obscured the mountains; hours went by before the sun could disperse those vapours and warm and purify the villages.

In New Mexico he always awoke a young man; not until he rose and began to shave did he realize that he was growing older. His first consciousness was a sense of the light dry wind blowing in through the windows, with the fragrance of hot sun and sage-brush and sweet clover; a wind that made one's body feel light and one's heart cry "To-day, to-day," like a child's.

Beautiful surroundings, the society of learned men, the charm of noble women, the graces of art, could not make up to him for the loss of those light-hearted mornings of the desert, for that wind that made one a boy again. He had noticed that this peculiar quality in the air of new countries vanished after they were tamed by man and made to bear harvests. Parts of Texas and Kansas that he had first known as open range had since been made into rich farming districts, and the air had quite lost that lightness, that dry aromatic odour. The moisture of plowed land, the heaviness of labour and growth and grain-bearing, utterly destroyed it; one could breathe that only on the bright edges of the world, on the great grass plains or the sage-brush desert.

That air would disappear from the whole earth in time, perhaps; but long after his day. He did not know just when it had become so necessary to him, but he had come back to die in exile for the sake of it. Something soft and wild and free, something that whispered to the ear on the pillow, lightened the heart, softly, softly picked the lock, slid the bolts, and released the prisoned spirit of man into the wind, into the blue and gold, into the morning, into the morning!

4

Father Latour arranged an order for his last days; if routine was necessary to him in health, it was even more so in sickness. Early in the morning Bernard came with hot water, shaved him, and helped him to bathe. They had brought nothing in from the country with them but clothing and linen, and the silver toilet articles the Olivares had given the Bishop so long ago; these thirty years he had washed his hands in that hammered basin. Morning prayers over, Magdalena came with his breakfast, and he sat in his easy-chair while she made his bed and arranged his room. Then he was ready to see visitors. The Archbishop came in for a few moments, when he was at home; the Mother Superior, the American doctor. Bernard read aloud to him the rest of the morning; St. Augustine, or the letters of Madame de Sevigné, or his favourite Pascal.

Sometimes, in the morning hours, he dictated to his young disciple certain facts about the old missions in the diocese; facts which he had come upon by chance and feared would be forgotten. He wished he could do this systematically, but he had not the strength. Those truths and fancies relating to a bygone time would probably be lost; the old legends and customs and superstitions were already dying out. He wished now that long ago he had had the leisure to write them down, that he could have arrested their flight by throwing about them the light and elastic mesh of the French tongue.

He had, indeed, for years, directed the thoughts of the young priests whom he instructed to the fortitude and devotion of those first missionaries, the Spanish friars; declaring that his own life, when he first came to New Mexico, was one of ease and comfort compared with theirs. If he had used to be abroad for weeks together on short rations, sleeping in the open, unable to keep his body clean, at least he had the sense of being in a friendly world, where by every man's fireside a welcome awaited him.

But the Spanish Fathers who came up to Zuñi, then went north to the Navajos, west to the Hopis, east to all the pueblos scattered between Albuquerque and Taos, they came into a hostile country, carrying little provisionment but their breviary and crucifix. When their mules were stolen by Indians, as often happened, they proceeded on foot, without a change of raiment, without food or water. A European could scarcely imagine such hardships. The old countries were worn to the shape of human life, made into an investiture, a sort of second body, for man. There the wild herbs and the wild fruits and the forest fungi were edible. The streams were sweet water, the trees afforded shade and shelter. But in the alkali deserts the water holes were poisonous, and the vegetation offered nothing to a starving man. Everything was dry, prickly, sharp; Spanish bayonet, juniper, greasewood, cactus; the lizard, the rattlesnake,—and man made cruel by a cruel life. Those early missionaries threw themselves naked upon the hard heart of a country that was calculated to try the endurance of giants. They thirsted in its deserts, starved among its rocks, climbed up and down its terrible canyons on stone-bruised feet, broke long fasts by unclean and repugnant food. Surely these endured *Hunger, Thirst, Cold, Nakedness,* of a kind beyond any conception St. Paul and his brethren could have had. Whatever the early Christians suffered, it all happened in that safe little Mediterranean world, amid the old manners, the old landmarks. If they endured martyrdom, they died among their brethren, their relics were piously preserved, their names lived in the mouths of holy men.

Riding with his Auvergnats to the old missions that had been scenes of martyrdom, the Bishop used to remind them that no man could know what triumphs of faith had happened there, where one white man met torture and death alone among so many infidels, or what visions and revelations God may have granted to soften that brutal end.

When, as a young man, Father Latour first went down into Old Mexico, to claim his See at the hands of the Bishop of Durango, he had met on his journey priests from the missions of Sonora and Lower California, who related many stories of the blessed experiences of the early Franciscan missionaries. Their way through the wilderness had blossomed with little miracles, it seemed. At one time, when the renowned Father Junípero Serra, and his two companions, were in danger of their lives from trying to cross a river at a treacherous point, a mysterious stranger appeared out of the rocks on the opposite shore, and calling to them in Spanish, told them to follow him to a point farther up the stream, where they forded in safety. When they begged to know his name, he evaded them and disappeared. At another time, they were traversing a great plain, and were famished for water and almost spent; a young horseman overtook them and gave them three ripe pomegranates, then galloped away. This fruit not only quenched their thirst, but revived and strengthened them as much as the most nourishing food could have done, and they completed their journey like fresh men.

One night in his travels through Durango, Father Latour was entertained at a great country estate where the resident chaplain happened to be a priest from one of the western missions; and he told a story of this same Father Junípero which had come down in his own monastery from the old times.

Father Junípero, he said, with a single companion, had once arrived at his monastery on foot, without provisions. The Brothers had welcomed the two in astonishment, believing it impossible that men could have crossed so great a stretch of desert in this naked fashion. The Superior questioned them as to whence they had come, and said the mission should not have allowed them to set off without a guide and without food. He marvelled how they could have got through alive. But Father Junípero replied that they had fared very well, and had been most agreeably entertained by a poor Mexican family on the way. At this a muleteer, who was bringing in wood for the Brothers, began to laugh, and said there was no house for twelve leagues, nor anyone at all living in the sandy waste through which they had come; and the Brothers confirmed him in this.

Then Father Junípero and his companion related fully their adventure. They had set out with bread and water for one day. But on the second day they had been travelling since dawn across a cactus desert and had begun to lose heart when, near sunset, they espied in the distance three great cottonwood trees, very tall in the declining light. Toward these they hastened. As they approached the trees, which were large and green and were shedding cotton freely, they observed an ass tied to a dead trunk which stuck up out of the sand. Looking about for the owner of the ass, they came upon a little Mexican house with an oven by the door and strings of red peppers hanging on the wall. When they called aloud, a venerable Mexican, clad in sheepskins, came out and greeted them kindly, asking them to stay the night. Going in with him, they observed that all was neat and comely, and the wife, a young woman of beautiful countenance, was stirring porridge by the fire. Her child, scarcely more than an infant and with no garment but his little shirt, was on the floor beside her, playing with a pet lamb.

They found these people gentle, pious, and well-spoken. The husband said they were shepherds. The priests sat at their table and shared their supper, and afterward read the evening prayers. They had wished to question the host about the country, and about his mode of life and where he found pasture for his flock, but they were overcome by a great and sweet weariness, and taking each a sheepskin provided him, they lay down upon the floor and sank into deep sleep. When they awoke in the morning they found all as before, and food set upon the table, but the family were absent, even to the pet lamb,— having gone, the Fathers supposed, to care for their flock.

When the Brothers at the monastery heard this account they were amazed, declaring that there were indeed three cottonwood trees growing together in the desert, a well-known landmark; but that if a settler had come, he must have come very lately. So Father Junípero and Father Andrea, his companion, with some of the Brothers and the scoffing muleteer, went back into the wilderness to prove the matter. The three tall trees they found, shedding their cotton, and the dead trunk to which the ass had been tied. But the ass was not there, nor any house, nor the oven by the door. Then the two Fathers sank down upon their knees in that blessed spot and kissed the earth, for they perceived what Family it was that had entertained them there.

Father Junípero confessed to the Brothers how from the moment he entered the house he had been strangely drawn to the child, and desired to take him in his arms, but that he kept near his mother. When the priest was reading the evening prayers the child sat upon the floor against his mother's knee, with the lamb in his lap, and the Father found it hard to keep his eyes upon his breviary. After prayers, when he bade his hosts good-night, he did indeed stoop over the little boy in blessing; and the child had lifted his hand, and with his tiny finger made the cross upon Father Junípero's forehead.

This story of Father Junípero's Holy Family made a strong impression upon the Bishop, when it was told him by the fireside of that great hacienda where he was a guest for the night. He had such an affection for that story, indeed, that he had allowed himself to repeat it on but two occasions; once to the nuns of Mother Philomène's convent in Riom, and once at a dinner given by Cardinal Mazzucchi, in Rome. There is always something charming in the idea of greatness returning to simplicity— the queen making hay among the country girls—but how much more endearing was the belief that They, after so many centuries of history and glory, should return to play Their first parts, in the persons of a humble Mexican family, the lowliest of the lowly, the poorest of the poor,— in a wilderness at the end of the world, where the angels could scarcely find Them!

5

After his *déjeuner* the old Archbishop made a pretence of sleeping. He requested not to be disturbed until dinner-time, and those long hours of solitude were precious to him. His bed was at the dark end of the room, where the shadows were restful to his eyes; on fair days the other end was full of sunlight, on grey days the light of the fire flickered along the wavy white walls. Lying so still that the bed-clothes over his body scarcely moved, with his hands resting delicately on the sheet beside him or upon his breast, the Bishop was living over his life. When he was otherwise motionless, the thumb of his right hand would sometimes gently touch a ring on his forefinger, an amethyst with an inscription cut upon it, *Auspice Maria,*— Father Vaillant's signet-ring; and then he was almost certainly thinking of Joseph; of their life together here, in this room . . . in Ohio beside the Great Lakes . . . as young men in Paris . . . as boys at Montferrand. There were many passages in their missionary life that he loved to recall; and how often and how fondly he recalled the beginning of it!

They were both young men in their twenties, curates to older priests, when there came to Clermont a Bishop from Ohio, a native of Auvergne, looking for volunteers for his missions in the West. Father Jean and Father Joseph heard him lecture at the Seminary, and talked with him in private. Before he left for the North, they had pledged themselves to meet him in Paris at a given date, to spend some weeks of preparation at the College for Foreign Missions in the rue du Bac, and then to sail with him from Cherbourg.

Both the young priests knew that their families would strongly oppose their purpose, so they resolved to reveal it to no one; to make no adieux, but to steal away disguised in civilian's clothes. They comforted each other by recalling that St. Francis Xavier, when he set forth as missionary to India, had stolen away like this; had *"passed the dwelling of his parents without saluting them,"* as they had learned at school; terrible words to a French boy.

Father Vaillant's position was especially painful; his father was a stern, silent man, long a widower, who loved his children with a jealous passion and had no life but in their lives. Joseph was the eldest child. The period between his resolve and its execution was a period of anguish for him. As the date set for their departure drew near, he grew thinner and paler than ever.

By agreement the two friends were to meet at dawn in a certain field outside Riom on the fateful day, and there await the *diligence* for Paris. Jean Latour, having made his decision and pledged himself, knew no wavering. On the appointed morning he stole out of his sister's house and took his way through the sleeping town to that mountain field, tip-tilted by reason of its steepness, just beginning to show a cold green in the heavy light of a cloudy daybreak. There he found his comrade in a miserable plight. Joseph had been abroad in the fields all night, wandering up and down, finding his purpose and losing it. His face was swollen with weeping. He shook with a chill, his voice was beyond his control.

"What shall I do, Jean? Help me!" he cried. "I cannot break my father's heart, and I cannot break the vow I have made to Heaven. I had rather die than do either. Ah, if I could but die of this misery, here, now!"

How clearly the old Archbishop could recall the scene; those two young men in the fields in the grey morning, disguised as if they were criminals, escaping by stealth from their homes. He had not known how to comfort his friend; it seemed to him that Joseph was suffering more than flesh could bear, that he was actually being torn in two by conflicting desires. While they were pacing up and down, arm-in-arm, they heard a hollow sound; the *diligence* rumbling down the mountain gorge. Joseph stood still and buried his face in his hands. The postilion's horn sounded.

"*Allons!*" said Jean lightly. "*L'invitation du voyage!* You will accompany me to Paris. Once we are there, if your father is not reconciled, we will get

Bishop F— to absolve you from your promise, and you can return to Riom. It is very simple."

He ran to the road-side and waved to the driver; the coach stopped. In a moment they were off, and before long Joseph had fallen asleep in his seat from sheer exhaustion. But he always said that if Jean Latour had not supported him in that hour of torment, he would have been a parish priest in the Puy-de-Dôme for the rest of his life.

Of the two young priests who set forth from Riom that morning in early spring, Jean Latour had seemed the one so much more likely to succeed in a missionary's life. He, indeed, had a sound mind in a sound body. During the weeks they spent at the College of Foreign Missions in the rue du Bac, the authorities had been very doubtful of Joseph's fitness for the hardships of the mission field. Yet in the long test of years it was that frail body that had endured more and accomplished more.

Father Latour often said that his diocese changed little except in boundaries. The Mexicans were always Mexicans, the Indians were always Indians. Santa Fé was a quiet backwater, with no natural wealth, no importance commercially. But Father Vaillant had been plunged into the midst of a great industrial expansion, where guile and trickery and honourable ambition all struggled together; a territory that developed by leaps and bounds and then experienced ruinous reverses. Every year, even after he was crippled, he travelled thousands of miles by stage and in his carriage, among the mountain towns that were now rich, now poor and deserted; Boulder, Gold Hill, Caribou, Cache-à-la-Poudre, Spanish Bar, South Park, up the Arkansas to Cache Creek and California Gulch.

And Father Vaillant had not been content to be a mere missionary priest. He became a promoter. He saw a great future for the Church in Colorado. While he was still so poor that he could not have a rectory or ordinary comfort to live in, he began buying up great tracts of land for the Church. He was able to buy a great deal of land for very little money, but that little had to be borrowed from banks at a ruinous rate of interest. He borrowed money to build schools and convents, and the interest on his debts ate him up. He made long begging trips through Ohio and Pennsylvania and Canada to raise money to pay this interest, which grew like a rolling snowball. He formed a land company, went abroad and floated bonds in France to raise money, and dishonest brokers brought reproach upon his name.

When he was nearly seventy, with one leg four inches shorter than the other, Father Vaillant, then first Bishop of Colorado, was summoned to Rome to explain his complicated finance before the Papal court,—and he had very hard work to satisfy the Cardinals.

When a dispatch was flashed into Santa Fé announcing Bishop Vaillant's death, Father Latour at once took the new railroad for Denver. But he could scarcely believe the telegram. He recalled the old nickname, *Trompe-la-Mort*, and remembered how many times before he had hurried across mountains and deserts, not daring to hope he would find his friend alive.

Curiously, Father Latour could never feel that he had actually been present at Father Joseph's funeral—or rather, he could not believe that Father Joseph was there. The shrivelled little old man in the coffin, scarcely larger than a monkey—that had nothing to do with Father Vaillant. He could see Joseph as clearly as he could see Bernard, but always as he was when they first came to New Mexico. It was not sentiment; that was the picture of Father Joseph his memory produced for him, and it did not produce any other. The funeral itself, he liked to remember—as a recognition. It was held under canvas, in the open air; there was not a building in Denver—in the whole Far West, for that matter,—big enough for his *Blanchet's* funeral. For two days before, the populations of villages and mining camps had been streaming down the mountains; they slept in wagons and tents and barns; they made a throng like a National Convention in the convent square. And a strange thing happened at that funeral:

Father Revardy, the French priest who had gone from Santa Fé to Colorado with Father Vaillant more than twenty years before, and had been with him ever since as his curate and Vicar, had been sent to France on business for his Bishop. While there, he was told by his physician that he had a fatal malady, and he at once took ship and hurried homeward, to make his report to Bishop Vaillant and to die in the harness. When he got as far as Chicago, he had an acute seizure and was taken to a Catholic hospital, where he lay very ill. One morning a nurse happened to leave a newspaper near his bed; glancing at it, Father saw an announcement of the death of the Bishop of Colorado. When the Sister returned, she found her patient dressed. He convinced her that he must be driven to the railway station at once. On reaching Denver he entered a carriage and asked to be taken to the Bishop's funeral. He arrived there when the services were nearly half over, and no one ever forgot the sight of this dying man, supported by the cab-driver and two priests, making his way through the crowd and dropping upon his knees beside the bier. A chair was brought for him, and for the rest of the ceremony he sat with his forehead resting against the edge of the coffin. When Bishop Vaillant was carried away to his tomb, Father Revardy was taken to the hospital, where he died a few days later. It was one more instance of the extraordinary personal devotion that Father Joseph had so often aroused and retained so long, in red men and yellow men and white.

6

During those last weeks of the Bishop's life he thought very little about death; it was the Past he was leaving. The future would take care of itself. But he had an intellectual curiosity about dying; about the changes that took place in a man's beliefs and scale of values. More and more life seemed to him an experience of the Ego, in no sense the Ego itself. This conviction, he believed, was something apart from his religious life; it was an enlightenment that came to him as a man, a human creature. And he noticed that he judged conduct differently now; his own and that of others. The mistakes of his life seemed unimportant; accidents that had occurred *en route*, like the shipwreck in Galveston harbour, or the runaway in which he was hurt when he was first on his way to New Mexico in search of his Bishopric.

He observed also that there was no longer any perspective in his memories. He remembered his winters with his cousins on the Mediterranean when he was a little boy, his student days in the Holy City, as clearly as he remembered the arrival of M. Molny and the building of his Cathedral. He was soon to have done with the calendared time, and it had already ceased to count for him. He sat in the middle of his own consciousness; none of his former states of mind were lost or outgrown. They were all within reach of his hand, and all comprehensible.

Sometimes, when Magdalena or Bernard came in and asked him a question, it took him several seconds to bring himself back to the present. He could see they thought his mind was failing; but it was only extraordinarily active in some other part of the great picture of his life—some part of which they knew nothing.

When the occasion warranted he could return to the present. But there was not much present left; Father Joseph dead, the Olivares both dead, Kit Carson dead, only the minor characters of his life remained in present time. One morning, several weeks after the Bishop came back to Santa Fé, one of the strong people of the old deep days of life did appear, not in memory but in the flesh, in the shallow light of the present; Eusabio the Navajo. Out on the Colorado Chiquito he had heard the word, passed on from one trading post to another, that the old Archbishop was failing, and the Indian came to Santa Fé. He, too, was an old man now. Once again their fine hands clasped. The Bishop brushed a drop of moisture from his eye.

"I have wished for this meeting, my friend. I had thought of asking you to come, but it is a long way."

The old Navajo smiled. "Not long now, any more. I come on the cars, Padre. I get on the cars at Gallup, and the same day I am here. You remember when we come together once to Santa Fé from my country? How long it take us? Two weeks, pretty near. Men travel faster now, but I do not know if they go to better things."

"We must not try to know the future, Eusabio. It is better not. And Manuelito?"

"Manuelito is well; he still leads his people."

Eusabio did not stay long, but he said he would come again to-morrow, as he had business in Santa Fé that would keep him for some days. He had no business there; but when he looked at Father Latour he said to himself, "It will not be long."

After he was gone, the Bishop turned to Bernard; "My son, I have lived to see two great wrongs righted; I have seen the end of black slavery, and I have seen the Navajos restored to their own country."

For many years Father Latour used to wonder if there would ever be an end to the Indian wars while there was one Navajo or Apache left alive. Too many traders and manufacturers made a rich profit out of that warfare; a political machine and immense capital were employed to keep it going.

7

The Bishop's middle years in New Mexico had been clouded by the persecution of the Navajos and their expulsion from their own country. Through his friendship with Eusabio he had become interested in the Navajos soon after he first came to his new diocese, and he admired them; they stirred his imagination. Though this nomad people were much slower to adopt white man's ways than the home-staying Indians who dwelt in pueblos, and were much more indifferent to missionaries and the white man's religion, Father Latour felt a superior strength in them. There was purpose and conviction behind their inscrutable reserve; something active and quick, something with an edge. The expulsion of the Navajos from their country, which had been theirs no man knew how long, had seemed to him an injustice that cried to Heaven. Never could he forget that terrible winter when they were being hunted down and driven by thousands from their own reservation to the Bosque Redondo, three hundred miles away on the Pecos River. Hundreds of them, men, women, and children, perished from hunger and cold on the way; their sheep and horses died from exhaustion crossing the mountains. None ever went willingly; they were driven by starvation and the bayonet; captured in isolated bands, and brutally deported.

It was his own misguided friend, Kit Carson, who finally subdued the last unconquered remnant of that people; who followed them into the depths of the Canyon de Chelly, whither they had fled from their grazing plains and pine forests to make their last stand. They were shepherds, with no property but their live-stock, encumbered by their women and children, poorly armed and with scanty ammunition. But this canyon had always before proved impenetrable to white troops. The Navajos believed it could not be taken. They believed that their old gods dwelt in the fastnesses of that canyon; like their Shiprock, it was an inviolate place, the very heart and centre of their life.

Carson followed them down into the hidden world between those towering walls of red sandstone, spoiled their stores, destroyed their deep-sheltered corn-fields, cut down the terraced peach orchards so dear to them. When they saw all that was sacred to them laid waste, the Navajos lost heart. They did not surrender; they simply ceased to fight, and were taken. Carson was a soldier under orders, and he did a soldier's brutal work. But the bravest of the Navajo chiefs he did not capture. Even after the crushing defeat of his people in the Canyon de Chelly, Manuelito was still at large. It was then that Eusabio came to Santa Fé to ask Bishop Latour to meet Manuelito at Zuñi. As a priest, the Bishop knew that it was indiscreet to consent to a meeting with this outlawed chief; but he was a man, too, and a lover of justice. The request came to him in such a way that he could not refuse it. He went with Eusabio.

Though the Government was offering a heavy reward for his person, living or dead, Manuelito rode off his own reservation down into Zuñi in broad daylight, attended by some dozen followers, all on wretched, half-starved horses. He had been in hiding out in Eusabio's country on the Colorado Chiquito.

It was Manuelito's hope that the Bishop would go to Washington and plead his people's cause before they were utterly destroyed. They asked nothing of the Government, he told Father Latour, but their religion, and their own land where they had lived from immemorial times. Their country, he explained, was a part of their religion; the two were inseparable. The Canyon de Chelly the Padre knew; in that canyon his people had lived when they were a small weak tribe; it had nourished and protected them; it was their mother. Moreover, their gods dwelt there—in those inaccessible white houses set in caverns up in the face of the cliffs, which were older than the white man's world, and which no living man had ever entered. Their gods were there, just as the Padre's God was in his church.

And north of the Canyon de Chelly was the Shiprock, a slender crag rising to a dizzy height, all alone out on a flat desert. Seen at a distance of fifty miles or so, that crag presents the figure of a one-masted fishing-boat under full sail, and the white man named it accordingly. But the Indian has another name; he believes that rock was once a ship of the air. Ages ago, Manuelito told the Bishop, that crag had moved through the air, bearing upon its summit the parents of the Navajo race from the place in the far north where all peoples were made,—and wherever it sank to earth was to be their land. It sank in a desert country, where it was hard for men to live. But they had found the Canyon de Chelly, where there was shelter and unfailing water. That canyon and the Shiprock were like kind parents to his people, places more sacred to them than churches, more sacred than any place is to the white man. How, then, could they go three hundred miles away and live in a strange land?

Moreover, the Bosque Redondo was down on the Pecos, far east of the Rio Grande. Manuelito drew a map in the sand, and explained to the Bishop how, from the very beginning, it had been enjoined that his people must never cross the Rio Grande on the east, or the Rio San Juan on the north, or the Rio Colorado on the west; if they did, the tribe would perish. If a great priest, like Father Latour, were to go to Washington and explain these things, perhaps the Government would listen.

Father Latour tried to tell the Indian that in a Protestant country the one thing a Roman priest could not do was to interfere in matters of Government. Manuelito listened respectfully, but the Bishop saw that he did not believe him. When he had finished, the Navajo rose and said:

"You are the friend of Christóbal, who hunts my people and drives them over the mountains to the Bosque Redondo. Tell your friend that he will never take me alive. He can come and kill me when he pleases. Two years ago I could not count my flocks; now I have thirty sheep and a few starving horses. My children are eating roots, and I do not care for my life. But my mother and my gods are in the West, and I will never cross the Rio Grande."

He never did cross it. He lived in hiding until the return of his exiled people. For an unforeseen thing happened:

The Bosque Redondo proved an utterly unsuitable country for the Navajos. It could have been farmed by irrigation, but they were nomad shepherds, not farmers. There was no pasture for their flocks. There was no firewood; they dug mesquite roots and dried them for fuel. It was an alkaline country, and hundreds of Indians died from bad water. At last the Government at Washington admitted its mistake—which governments seldom do. After five years of exile, the remnant of the Navajo people were permitted to go back to their sacred places.

In 1875 the Bishop took his French architect on a pack trip into Arizona to show him something of the country before he returned to France, and he had the pleasure of seeing the Navajo horsemen riding free over their great plains again. The two Frenchmen went as far as the Canyon de Chelly to behold the strange cliff ruins; once more crops were growing down at the bottom of the world between the towering sandstone walls; sheep were grazing under the magnificent cottonwoods and drinking at the streams of sweet water; it was like an Indian Garden of Eden.

Now, when he was an old man and ill, scenes from those bygone times, dark and bright, flashed back to the Bishop: the terrible faces of the Navajos waiting at the place on the Rio Grande where they were being ferried across into exile; the long streams of survivors going back to their own country, driving their scanty flocks, carrying their old men and their children. Memories, too, of that time he had spent with Eusabio on the Little Colorado, in the early spring, when the lambing season was not yet over,—dark horsemen riding across the sands with orphan lambs in their arms—a young Navajo woman, giving a lamb her breast until a ewe was found for it.

"Bernard," the old Bishop would murmur, "God has been very good to let me live to see a happy issue to those old wrongs. I do not believe, as I once did, that the Indian will perish. I believe that God will preserve him."

8

The American doctor was consulting with Archbishop S—— and the Mother Superior. "It is his heart that is the trouble now. I have been giving him small doses to stimulate it, but they no longer have any effect. I scarcely dare increase them; it might be fatal at once. But that is why you see such a change in him."

The change was that the old man did not want food, and that he slept, or seemed to sleep, nearly all the time. On the last day of his life his condition was pretty generally known. The Cathedral was full of people all day long, praying for him; nuns and old women, young men and girls, coming and going. The sick man had received the Viaticum early in the morning. Some of the Tesuque Indians, who had been his country neighbours, came into Santa Fé and sat all day in the Archbishop's court-yard listening for news of him; with them was Eusabio the Navajo. Fructosa and Tranquilino, his old servants, were with the supplicants in the Cathedral.

The Mother Superior and Magdalena and Bernard attended the sick man. There was little to do but to watch and pray, so peaceful and painless was his repose. Sometimes it was sleep, they knew from his relaxed features; then his face would assume personality, consciousness, even though his eyes did not open.

Toward the close of the day, in the short twilight after the candles were lighted, the old Bishop seemed to become restless, moved a little, and began to murmur; it was in the French tongue, but Bernard, though he caught some words, could make nothing of them. He knelt beside the bed: "What is it, Father? I am here."

He continued to murmur, to move his hands a little, and Magdalena thought he was trying to ask for something, or to tell them something. But in reality the bishop was not there at all; he was standing in a tip-tilted green field among his native mountains, and he was trying to give consolation to a young man who was being torn in two before his eyes by the desire to go and the necessity to stay. He was trying to forge a new Will in that devout and exhausted priest; and the time was short, for the *diligence* for Paris was already rumbling down the mountain gorge.

When the Cathedral bell tolled just after dark, the Mexican population of Santa Fé fell upon their knees, and all American Catholics as well. Many others who did not kneel prayed in their hearts. Eusabio and the Tesuque boys went quietly away to tell their people; and the next morning the old Archbishop lay before the high altar in the church he had built.

Related Readings

Willa Cather	On *Death Comes for the Archbishop*	letter to the editor	171
Alfonso Ortiz	Through Tewa Eyes: Origins	magazine article	176
Luci Tapahonso	In 1864	poem	182
John Donne	Holy Sonnet 167	poem	186
Leslie Marmon Silko	Where Mountain Lion Lay Down with Deer	poem	187
Dennis L. Coello	American Odyssey: Cycling the Santa Fe Trail	magazine article	189

On Death Comes for the Archbishop

Willa Cather

In 1927 Willa Cather wrote to the editor of The Commonweal, *an independent Catholic journal of opinion. Cather used the magazine as a platform to answer questions about the historical accuracy of the novel and her sources of information.*

Unable to reply personally to the hundreds of letters Miss Cather received asking her in how far Death Comes for the Archbishop was historical, and what were her sources of information, she wrote the following letter to The Commonweal:

To THE EDITOR OF *The Commonweal:*—You have asked me to give you a short account of how I happened to write *Death Comes for the Archbishop.*

When I first went into the Southwest some fifteen years ago, I stayed there for a considerable period of time. It was then much harder to get about than it is today. There were no automobile roads and no hotels off the main lines of railroad. One had to travel by wagon and carry a camp outfit. One travelled slowly, and had plenty of time for reflection. It was then very difficult to find anyone who would tell me anything about the country, or even about the roads. One of the most intelligent and inspiring persons I found in my travels was a Belgian priest, Father Haltermann, who lived with his sister in the parsonage behind the beautiful old church at Santa Cruz, New Mexico, where he raised fancy poultry and sheep and had a wonderful vegetable and flower garden. He was a florid, full-bearded farmer priest, who drove about among his eighteen Indian missions with a spring wagon and a pair of mules. He knew a great deal about the country and the Indians and their traditions. He went home during the war to serve as a chaplain in the French Army, and when I last heard of him he was an invalid.

The longer I stayed in the Southwest, the more I felt that the story of the Catholic Church in that country was the most interesting of all its stories. The old mission churches, even those which were abandoned and in ruins, had a moving reality about them; the hand carved beams and joists, the utterly unconventional frescoes, the countless fanciful figures of the saints, no two of them alike, seemed a direct expression of some very real and lively human feeling. They were all fresh, individual, first-hand. Almost every one of those many remote little adobe churches in the mountains or in the desert had something lovely that was its own. In lonely, sombre villages in the mountains the church decorations were sombre, the martyrdoms bloodier, the grief of the Virgin more agonized, the figure of Death more terrifying. In warm, gentle valleys everything about the churches was milder. I used to wish there were some written account of the old times when those churches were built; but I soon felt that no record of them could be as real as they are themselves. They are their own story, and it is foolish convention that we must have everything interpreted for us in written language. There are other ways of telling what one feels, and the people who built and decorated those many, many little churches found their way and left their message.

May I say here that within the last few years some of the newer priests down in that country have been taking away from those old churches their old homely images and decoration, which have a definite artistic and historic value, and replacing them by conventional, factory-made church furnishings from New York? It is a great pity. All Catholics will be sorry about it, I think, when it is too late, when all those old paintings and images and carved doors that have so much feeling and individuality are gone—sold to some collector in New York or Chicago, where they mean nothing.

During the twelve years that followed my first year in New Mexico and Arizona I went back as often as I could, and the story of the Church and the Spanish missionaries was always what most interested me; but I hadn't the most remote idea of trying to write about it. I was working on things of a very different nature, and any story of the Church in the Southwest was certainly the business of some Catholic writer, and not mine at all.

Meanwhile Archbishop Lamy, the first Bishop of New Mexico, had become a sort of invisible personal friend. I had heard a great many interesting stories about him from very old Mexicans and traders who still remembered him, and I never passed the life-sized bronze of him which stands under a locust tree before the Cathedral in Santa Fé without wishing that I could learn more about a pioneer churchman who looked so well-bred and distinguished. In his pictures one felt the same thing, something fearless and fine and very, very well-bred—something that spoke of race. What I felt curious about was the daily life of such a man in a crude frontier society.

Two years ago, in Santa Fé, that curiosity was gratified. I came upon a book printed years ago on a country press at Pueblo, Colorado: *The Life of the Right Reverend Joseph P. Machebeuf,* by William Joseph Howlett, a priest who had worked with Father Machebeuf in Denver. The book is an admirable piece of work, revealing as much about Father Lamy as about Father Machebeuf, since the two men were so closely associated from early youth. Father Howlett had gone to France and got his information about Father Machebeuf's youth direct from his sister, Philomene. She gave him her letters from Father Machebeuf, telling all the little details of his life in New Mexico, and Father Howlett inserted dozens of them, splendidly translated, into his biography. At last I found out what I wanted to know about how the country and the people of New Mexico seemed to those first missionary priests from France. Without these letters in Father Howlett's book to guide me, I would certainly never have dared to write my book. Of course, many of the incidents I used were experiences of my own, but in these letters I learned how experiences very similar to them affected Father Machebeuf and Father Lamy.

My book was a conjunction of the general and the particular, like most works of the imagination. I had all my life wanted to do something in the style of legend, which is absolutely the reverse of dramatic treatment. Since I first saw the Puvis de Chavannes frescoes of the life of Saint Geneviève in my student days, I have wished that I could try something a little like that in prose; something with accent, with none of the artificial elements of composition. In the Golden Legend the martyrdoms of the saints are no more dwelt upon than are the trivial incidents of their lives; it is as though all human experiences, measured against one supreme spiritual experience, were of about the same importance. The essence of such writing is not to hold the note, not to use an incident for all there is in it—but to touch and pass on. I felt that such writing would be a kind of discipline in these days when the "situation" is made to count for so much in writing, when the general tendency is to force things up. In this kind of writing the mood is the thing—all the little figures and stories are mere improvisations that come out of it. What I got from Father Machebeuf's letters was the mood, the spirit in which they accepted the accidents and hardships of a desert country, the joyful energy that kept them going. To attempt to convey this hardihood of spirit one must use language a little stiff, a little formal, one must not be afraid of the old trite phraseology of the frontier. Some of those time-worn phrases I used as the note from the piano by which the violinist tunes his instrument. Not that there was much difficulty in keeping the pitch. I did not sit down to write the book until the feeling of it had so teased me that I could not get on with other things. The writing of it took only a few months, because the book had all been lived many times before it was written, and the happy mood in which I began it never paled. It was like going back and playing the early composers after a surfeit of modern music.

One friendly reviewer says that to write the book I soaked myself in Catholic lore; perhaps it would have been better if I had. But too much information often makes one pompous, and it's rather deadening. Some things I had to ask about. I had no notion of the manner in which a missionary from the new world would be received by the Pope, so I simply asked an old friend, Father Dennis Fitzgerald, the resident priest in Red Cloud, Nebraska, where my parents live. He was a student in Rome in his youth, so I asked him to tell me something about the procedure of a formal audience with the Pope. There again I had to exercise self-restraint, for he told me such interesting things that I was strongly tempted to make Father Vaillant's audience stand out too much, to particularize it. Knowledge that one hasn't got first-hand is a dangerous thing for a writer, it comes too easily!

Writing this book (the title, by the way, which has caused a good deal of comment, was simply taken from Holbein's *Dance of Death*) was like a happy vacation from life, a return to childhood, to early memories. As a writer I had the satisfaction of working in a special genre which I had long wished to try. As a human being, I had the pleasure of paying an old debt of gratitude to the valiant men whose life and work had given me so many hours of pleasant reflection in far-away places where certain unavoidable accidents and physical discomforts gave me a feeling of close kinship with them. In the main, I followed the life story of the two Bishops very much as it was, though I used many of my own experiences, and some of my father's. In actual fact, of course, Bishop Lamy died first of the two friends, and it was Bishop Machebeuf who went to his funeral. Often have I heard from the old people how he broke down when he rose to speak and was unable to go on.

I am amused that so many of the reviews of this book begin with the statement: "This book is hard to classify." Then why bother? Many more assert vehemently that it is not a novel. Myself, I prefer to call it a narrative. In this case I think that term more appropriate. But a novel, it seems to me, is merely a work of imagination in which a writer tries to present the experiences and emotions of a group of people by the light of his own. That is what he really does, whether his method is "objective" or "subjective."

I hope that I have told you what you wished to know about my book, and I remain,

Very sincerely yours,
Willa Cather

November 23, 1927

In his review of *Death Comes for the Archbishop*, Michael Williams wrote in *The Commonweal*:

"Her [Willa Cather's] book is a wonderful proof of the power of the true artist to penetrate and understand and to express things not part of the equipment of the artist as a person. Miss Cather is not a Catholic, yet certainly no Catholic American writer that I know of has ever written so many pages so steeped in spiritual knowledge and understanding of Catholic motives and so sympathetically illustrative of the wonder and beauty of Catholic mysteries, as she has done in this book."

Alfonso Ortiz

Through Tewa Eyes: Origins

The native people of New Mexico in Death Comes for the Archbishop *are the Tewas. This article by a Tewa Pueblo Indian provides insight into their customs and beliefs.*

I do not remember the day, of course, but I know what happened. Four days after I was born in the Pueblo Indian village of San Juan in the Rio Grande Valley in New Mexico, the "umbilical cord-cutting mother" and her assistant came to present me to the sun and to give me a name. They took me from the house just as the sun's first rays appeared over the Sangre de Cristo Mountains. The cord-cutting mother proffered me and two perfect ears of corn, one blue and one white, to the six sacred directions. A prayer was said:

Here is a child who has been given to us. Let us bring him to manhood. . . . You who are dawn youths and dawn maidens. You who are winter spirits. You who are summer spirits. . . . Take therefore. . . . Give him good fortune, we ask of you.

Now the name was given. It was not the name at the head of this story. It was my Tewa name, a thing of power. Usually such a name evokes either nature—the mountains or the hills or the season—or a ceremony under way at the time of the birth. By custom such a name is shared only within the community, and with those we know well. Thus, in the eyes of my Tewa people, I was "brought in out of the darkness," where I had no identity. Thus I became a child of the Tewa. My world is the Tewa world. It is different from your world.

Consider the question of the origin of Native American peoples. Archaeologists will tell you that we came at least 12,000 years ago from Asia, crossing the Bering land bridge, then spreading over the two American continents. These archaeologists have dug countless holes in the earth looking for spearpoints, bones, traces of fires; they have subjected these objects to sophisticated dating analysis—seeking to prove or disprove a hypothesis or date. I know of their work. I too have been to Soviet Asia and seen cave art and an old ceremonial costume remarkably similar to some found in America. But a Tewa is not so interested in the work of archaeologists.

A Tewa is interested in our own story of our origin, for it holds all that we need to know about our people, and how one should live as a human. The story defines our society. It tells me who I am, where I came from, the boundaries of my world, what kind of order exists within it; how suffering, evil, and death came into this world; and what is likely to happen to *me* when I die.

Let me tell you that story:
> *Yonder in the north there is singing on the lake. Cloud maidens dance on the shore. There we take our being.*
> *Yonder in the north cloud beings rise. They ascend onto cloud blossoms. There we take our being.*
> *Yonder in the north rain stands over the land. . . . Yonder in the north stands forth at twilight the arc of a rainbow. There we have our being.*

Our ancestors came from the north. Theirs was not a journey to be measured in centuries, for it was as much a journey of the spirit as it was a migration of a people. The Tewa know not when the journey southward began or when it ended, but we do know where it began, how it proceeded, and where it ended. We are unconcerned about time in its historical dimensions, but we will recall in endless detail the features of the 12 places our ancestors stopped.

We point to these places to show that the journey did indeed take place. This is the only proof a Tewa requires. And each time a Tewa recalls a place where they paused, for whatever length of time, every feature of the earth and sky comes vividly to life, and the journey itself lives again.

AT THE BEGINNING of all beginnings our ancestors came up out of the earth, until they were living beneath Sandy Place Lake to the north. The world under the lake was like this one, but dark. Spirits, people, and animals lived together; death was unknown.

Among the spirits were the first mothers of all the Tewa, known as Blue Corn Woman Near to Summer and White Corn Maiden Near to Ice. These mothers asked one of the men present to go forth and explore the way by which the people might leave the lake.

After many adventures and struggles he returned to the people, announcing his arrival with the call of a fox. He came now as Mountain Lion or Hunt Chief. The people rejoiced, saying, "We have been accepted."

They left the lake and entered the land.

That the Tewa see all life as beginning within the earth, like the corn plant that has sustained us for centuries, is manifest in our sacred places: The kiva, the ceremonial center, which represents the primordial home under the lake; the "earth mother earth navel middle place" in every village; and our mountaintop shrines—"earth navels"—shaped of stones or boulders.

These trace back to the first permanent habitations of the Pueblo people.

The canyons, cliffs, and mesa tops of the Four Corners area of the Southwest hold evidence that, at least by the fifth century anno Domini (as the white man reckons time), the Pueblo people did, indeed, begin life within the earth. The habitations they constructed were circular pit houses, dug wholly or mostly underground and covered with branches and dirt. Entrance ramps opened to the southeast, the direction of the rising sun during the colder months of the year. To enter the pit house, then, was to enter the earth, and to enter the earth was to return to one of the two sources of all life through the opening that connected it with the other source, the sun.

These pit-house people lived within the womb of mother earth while also drawing sustenance from the sun father. A small round hole was also dug and carefully protected on the floor of their pit house to remind them of their original emergence from within the earth. They termed such a hole "earth germinating mother earth navel middle place"—the origin of the sacred place in the plazas of our villages today.

From the outside these pit houses resembled nothing more than giant rounded anthills. Yet their form would take on profound meaning.

IN TIME the pit-house people emerged to build, aboveground, rectangular house blocks, but they retained the basic shape of their pit house by building kivas, or ceremonial chambers, one of which was always attached to each house block. These were built underground and to the southeast. The kiva was no longer entered through a sloping ramp but through a hole in the roof. The old rampway was now represented by a deeply recessed wall, still located in the southeast part of the kiva. This new structure resembled an old-fashioned keyhole so much that it is called a keyhole-shaped kiva by archaeologists.

Southeast of the kiva was the refuse depositing place, where the dead were buried. The positioning of the dead closest to the direction of the sunrise reflects a recognition by the Pueblo people that the sun father is both the giver and the taker of life. What he gives he also takes back, eventually. The three parts—house block, kiva, and refuse dump/cemetery—became standard.

And the kiva, in its central position, came to mediate between the living and the dead. Here the living may perform rituals addressed to the dead and, hence, communicate with them. In later times there were great dramatic performances in which the living personified the spirits of the dead in these kivas.

Finally the villages became multistoried house blocks resembling fortresses. This presented a dilemma to the people: The buildings blocked the rising sun's rays from the dead buried outside. The old keyhole kiva must give way.

Today the kiva may be a rectangular room in the house block, but the old form is retained; an opening provides an unobstructed channel toward the sunrise, representing the lifeline into the village.

The people also took the shape of the pit house and old kiva to the mountaintops, creating a keyhole form with stones, with the lower end of the keyhole opened toward the sunrise. Only the form reminded one that it represented what was once an underground habitation and later a religious sanctum. The Tewa continue to make pilgrimages to the mountain earth navels, for these are places of great power: They provide the Tewa with a way of rediscovering who we are and of renewing our ties to our beginnings. They represent ongoing lifelines to sustain all creation. And—through the centuries when the Spanish and other peoples dominated the Tewa—these places have provided a tenacious symbol of survival.

Our genesis story establishes another vital aspect of our lives. Remember my naming ceremony: There were two women attending, two ears of corn offered with me to the sun. This duality is basic to understanding our behavior.

When the Tewa came onto land, the Hunt Chief took an ear of blue corn and handed it to one of the other men and said: "You are to lead and care for all the people during the summer." To another man he handed an ear of white corn and told him: "You shall lead and care for the people during the winter." This is how the Summer and Winter Chiefs were instituted.

The Hunt Chief then divided the people between the two chiefs. As they moved south down the Rio Grande, the Summer People traveled on the west side of the river, the Winter People on the east side.

The Summer People lived by agriculture, the Winter People by hunting.

From this time, the story tells us, the Tewa have been divided during their lives into moieties—Winter People, Summer People. Still today a Summer Chief guides us seven months of the year, during the agricultural cycle; a Winter Chief during the five months of hunting. There are special rituals, dances, costumes, and colors attached to each moiety. Everything that has symbolic significance to the Tewa is classified in dualities: Games, plants, and diseases are hot or cold, winter or summer. Some persons or things, like healers, are of the middle, mediating between the two. This gives order to our lives.

A child is incorporated into his moiety through the water-giving ceremony during his first year. The Winter Chief conducts his rite in October; the Summer Chief in late February or March. The ceremony is held in a sanctuary at the chief's home. There are an altar, a sand painting, and various symbols; the chief and his assistants dress in white buckskin. A final character appears, preceded by the call of a fox, as in the creation story. It is the Hunt Chief.

A female assistant holds the child; the moiety chief recites a short prayer and administers a drink of the sacred medicinal water from an abalone shell, thereby welcoming the child into the moiety.

The third rite in a child's life—water pouring—comes between the ages of six and ten and is held within the moiety. It marks the transition from the carefree, innocent state of early childhood to the status of adult, one of the Dry Food People. For four days the boys are made to carry a load of firewood they have chopped themselves, and girls a basket of cornmeal they have ground themselves, to the homes of their sponsors.

A sponsor instructs each child in the beliefs and practices of the village. On the fourth night, the deities come to the kiva, and the child may go to watch. Afterward, the sponsor bathes the child, pouring water over him. From this time, the child is given duties judged proper for his sex.

A finishing ritual a few years later brings the girls and boys to adulthood. For the boys it is particularly meaningful, for they now become eligible to assist and participate in the coming of the gods in their moiety's kiva. Thus the bonds of the moiety are further strengthened.

IT IS AT DEATH that the bond of moiety is broken and the solidarity of the whole society emphasized again. This echoes the genesis story, for after the people had divided into two for their journey from the lake, they came together again when they arrived at their destination.

When a Tewa dies, relatives dress the corpse. The moccasins are reversed—for the Tewa believe everything in the afterlife is reversed from this life. There is a Spanish Catholic wake, a Requiem Mass, then the trip to the cemetery. There the priest completes the church's funeral rites: the sprinkling of holy water, a prayer, a handful of dirt thrown into the grave. Then all non-Indians leave.

A bag containing the clothing of the deceased is now placed under his head as a pillow, along with other personal possessions. When the grave is covered, a Tewa official tells the survivors that the deceased has gone to the place "of endless cicada singing," that he will be happy, and he admonishes them not to let the loss divide the home.

During the four days following death, the soul, or Dry Food Who Is No Longer, is believed to wander about in this world in the company of the ancestors. These four days produce a time of unease. There is the fear among relatives that the soul may become lonely and return to take one of them for company. Children are deemed most susceptible. The house itself must not be left unoccupied.

The uneasiness ends on the fourth night, when relatives gather again to perform the releasing rite. There are rituals with tobacco, a piece of charcoal, a series of four lines drawn on the floor. A pottery bowl, used in his naming ceremony long ago and cherished by him all his life, is broken, or "killed." Then a prayer reveals the purpose of the symbols:

We have muddied the waters for you [the smoke]. We have cast shadows between us [the charcoal]. We have made steep gullies between us [the lines]. Do not, therefore, reach for even a hair on our heads. Rather, help us attain that which we are always seeking: Long life, that our children may grow, abundant game, the raising of crops. . . . Now you must go, for you are now free.

With the soul released, all breathe a sigh of relief. They wash their hands. As each finishes, he says, "May you have life." The others respond, "Let it be so." Everyone now eats.

The Tewa begin and end life as one people; we call the life cycle *poeh*, or emergence path. As a Tewa elder told me:

"In the beginning we were one. Then we divided into Summer People and Winter People; in the end we came together again as we are today."

This is the path of our lives.

Luci Tapahonso | # In 1864

> In 1864 over eight thousand Navajos were relocated by the U.S. government and forced to walk three hundred miles from Dinetah* to Bosque Redondo in New Mexico. There, more than two thousand died of illness and starvation. Only in 1868 did the government allow the survivors to return to their homeland.

While the younger daughter slept, she dreamt of mountains,
the wide blue sky above, and friends laughing.

We talked as the day wore on. The stories and highway beneath
became a steady hum. The center lines were a blurred guide.
5   As we neared the turn to Fort Sumner,‡ I remembered this story:

A few winters ago, he worked as an electrician on a crew
installing power lines on the western plains of New Mexico.
He stayed in his pickup camper, which was connected to a
   generator.
The crew parked their trucks together and built a fire in the center.
10 The nights were cold and there weren't any trees to break the wind.
It snowed off and on, a quiet, still blanket. The land was like
he had imagined from the old stories—flat and dotted with shrubs.
The arroyos and washes cut through the soft dirt.
They were unsuspectingly deep.
15 During the day, the work was hard and the men were exhausted.
In the evenings, some went into the nearby town to eat and drink

---

* "Dinetah" means "Navajo country" or "homeland of The People."
‡ Fort Sumner was also called "Bosque Redondo," owing to its location.

a few beers. He fixed a small meal for himself and tried to relax.
Then at night, he heard cries and moans carried by the wind
and blowing snow. He heard the voices wavering and rising
20   in the darkness. He would turn over and pray, humming songs
he remembered from his childhood. The songs returned to him
as easily as if he had heard them that very afternoon.
He sang for himself, his family, and the people whose spirits
lingered on the plains, in the arroyos, and in the old windswept
    plants.
25   No one else heard the thin wailing.
After the third night, he unhooked his camper, signed his time card,
and started the drive north to home. He told the guys,
"Sure, the money's good. But I miss my kids and it sure gets lonely
out here for a family man." He couldn't stay there any longer.
30   The place contained the pain and cries of his relatives,
the confused and battered spirits of his own existence.

After we stopped for a Coke and chips, the storytelling resumed:

My aunt always started the story saying, "you are here
because of what happened to your great–grandmother long ago."

35   They began rounding up the people in the fall.
Some were lured into surrendering by offers of food, clothes,
and livestock. So many of us were starving and suffering
that year because the bilagáana[*] kept attacking us.
Kit Carson and his army had burned all the fields,
40   and they killed our sheep right in front of us.
We couldn't believe it. I covered my face and cried.
All my life, we had sheep. They were like our family.
It was then I knew our lives were in great danger.

We were all so afraid of that man, Redshirt,[‡] and his army.
45   Some people hid in the foothills of the Chuska Mountains
and in Canyon de Chelly. Our family talked it over,
and we decided to go to this place. What would our lives
be like without sheep, crops, and land? At least, we thought
we would be safe from gunfire and our family would not starve.

---

[*] "Bilagáana" is the Navajo word for Anglos.
[‡] Kit Carson's name was "Redshirt" in Navajo.

50 The journey began, and the soldiers were all around us.
All of us walked, some carried babies. Little children and the elderly
stayed in the middle of the group. We walked steadily each day,
stopping only when the soldiers wanted to eat or rest.
We talked among ourselves and cried quietly.
55 We didn't know how far it was or even where we were going.
All that was certain was that we were leaving Dinetah, our home.
As the days went by, we grew more tired, and soon,
the journey was difficult for all of us, even the military.
And it was they who thought all this up.

60 We had such a long distance to cover.
Some old people fell behind, and they wouldn't let us go back to
   help them.
It was the saddest thing to see—my heart hurts so to remember that.
Two women were near the time of the births of their babies,
and they had a hard time keeping up with the rest.
65 Some army men pulled them behind a huge rock, and we screamed
   out loud
when we heard the gunshots. The women didn't make a sound,
but we cried out loud for them and their babies.
I felt then that I would not live through everything.

When we crossed the Rio Grande, many people drowned.
70 We didn't know how to swim—there was hardly any water deep
   enough
to swim in at home. Some babies, children, and some of the older
   men
and women were swept away by the river current.
We must not ever forget their screams and the last we saw of
   them—
hands, a leg, or strands of hair floating.

75 There were many who died on the way to Hwééldi.* All the way
we told each other, "We will be strong as long as we are together."
I think that was what kept us alive. We believed in ourselves
and the old stories that the holy people had given us.
"This is why," she would say to us. "This is why we are here.
80 Because our grandparents prayed and grieved for us."

---

* Hwééldi is the Navajo name for Fort Sumner.

The car hums steadily, and my daughter is crying softly.
Tears stream down her face. She cannot speak. Then I tell her that
it was at Bosque Redondo the people learned to use flour and now
fry bread is considered to be the "traditional" Navajo bread.
85 It was there that we acquired a deep appreciation for strong coffee.
The women began to make long, tiered calico skirts
and fine velvet shirts for the men. They decorated their dark velvet
blouses with silver dimes, nickels, and quarters.
They had no use for money then.
90 It is always something to see—silver flashing in the sun
against dark velvet and black, black hair.

John Donne

Holy Sonnet 167

The speaker of this poem does not fear death. Like Father Latour, he sees death as a natural part of life and believes that he will wake to an eternal afterlife.

Death be not proud, though some have called thee
Mighty and dreadfull, for, thou art not soe,
For, those, whom thou think'st, thou dost overthrow,
Die not, poore death, nor yet canst thou kill mee;
5 From rest and sleepe, which but thy pictures bee,
Much pleasure, then from thee, much more must flow,
And soonest our best men with thee doe goe,
Rest of their bones, and soules deliverie.
Thou'art slave to Fate, chance, kings, and desperate men,
10 And dost with poyson, warre, and sicknesse dwell,
And poppie,'or charmes can make us sleepe as well,
And better then thy stroake; why swell'st thou then?
One short sleepe past, wee wake eternally,
And death shall be no more, Death thou shalt die.

Leslie Marmon Silko

Where Mountain Lion Lay Down with Deer

Leslie Marmon Silko, a distinguished Pueblo author, wrote this lament for a lost people and culture.

      I climb the black rock mountain
      stepping from day to day
                  silently.
      I smell the wind for my ancestors
5   pale blue leaves
         crushed wild mountain smell.
      Returning
        up the gray stone cliff
        where I descended
10   a thousand years ago
      Returning to faded black stone
      where mountain lion lay down with deer.
      It is better to stay up here
                  watching wind's reflection
15   in tall yellow flowers.
      The old ones who remember me are gone
         the old songs are all forgotten
      and the story of my birth.

                    How I danced in snow-frost moonlight
20   distant stars to the end of the Earth,
                    How I swam away
                                in freezing mountain water
                                narrow mossy canyon tumbling down
                                        out of the mountain
25   out of the deep canyon
                                            stone
                                    down
                                        the memory
                                                spilling out
                                                into world.

Dennis L. Coello

American Odyssey: Cycling the Santa Fe Trail

This article compares the experience of traveling along the Santa Fe Trail on bicycle to the experience of William Becknell, who forged the trail in the 1800s.

We were close to Dodge City, Kansas—roughly the halfway point on our 1,000-mile winter ride from New Mexico to Missouri. On the north side of the road a sign read "Santa Fe Trail Tracks—1822-1872." We dismounted and climbed the hill. Overhead were gray, chilly skies, and behind us lay the wide Arkansas River valley. What little water there was reflected the sky's somber hues. The cottonwoods on either bank reminded me of old Civil War photographs. In all it was a scene which might have been depressing—but instead my heart raced as I neared the top of the hill. There, before me, were the century-old physical traces of those who had traveled before.

A half-hour later we sat eating lunch on the edge of one of these trail ruts, as a few cold drops of November rain began to fall. On other rides such weather might have ruined the day—but not now. For my friend and tour companion, Larry Miller, and I had chosen to experience the Santa Fe Trail as it was known to the first travelers. And all the elements seemed thereby miraculously transformed. Gray skies were not wished blue, nor Kansas prairies desired to be mountains instead. We read the diaries of those who once sat where we did now, 100-year-old entries that described the same landforms and weather conditions. And unlike rides of only pleasant days and pretty scenery, the thrill of such a time-leap remains forever.

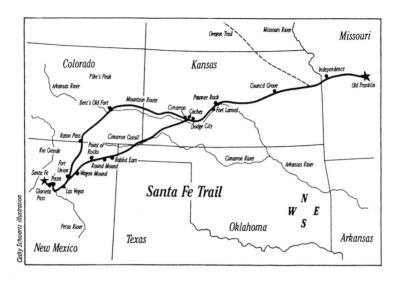

Back to the Land

I took my first cross-country ride in '65, and in the interim have filled the years with miles of scenic tours. But none compare to the two historic trails I've covered recently—Santa Fe, and the 3,000-mile Lewis and Clark Expedition. History, of course, could not foresee the best routes for today's traveler, who will sometimes be forced to endure a busy stretch of chuckholed highway, or rough riding on roads of dirt. But if you love cycling, if you're up for a taste of adversity, and if you care to learn our nation's history in perhaps the most unforgettable manner possible, then cycle-touring along America's trails is for you. Traveling by bike gives you a chance to be close to the land and to see firsthand the landmarks left by pioneers. For me, there is no better way to leap across the centuries.

Trail Beginnings

When William Becknell set out from Franklin, Missouri, armed with trinkets and supplies to trade with the Comanche Indians in 1821, he had no idea what lay across the Arkansas River. Reports of traders, imprisoned by angry Spaniards who had no wish for their territory to be invaded, had discouraged many adventurers.

But the soldiers who finally met up with Becknell brought comforting news: Mexico had won her independence from Spain and would welcome Americans in the city of Santa Fe. Thus the trail was forged in the years to come by the sweat of pioneers who toiled across the prairies in wagons.

The traces of their hardship still remain. I remember an elderly couple in Nevada who eagerly whisked us into their car and sped breakneck across rocky terrain just so I could photograph some of the original wagon ruts before the sunset faded.

We met others along the way who were just as proud of their heritage. The Santa Fe Trail goes back several generations, and we often met people who descended from the original homesteaders.

I recall a woman in a cafe in Canton, Kansas, who spoke of her forebears' place in trail history, then directed me to a nearby cemetery.

"There are three generations of us here already," she said, pointing to some faded and crumbling markers, "and there are three generations of my family that are walking around in town today. Eventually we'll join our ancestors here, but the trail will still remain."

I suddenly realized the land's history is not only found in its scarred and pitted surface, but in the hearts and stories of its people.

The Journey Begins

We had decided, because of prevailing winds, to follow the trail from west to east. Our first destination, Santa Fe, was a pleasant shock.

The combination of adobe dwellings, narrow streets, and pure blue skies gave the city a distinctly European flavor. Spoken English is often laced with the quick, melodious native Spanish tongue, while the mixture of American, Spanish, and Indian cultures is obvious in the physical features of both the town and its people. Plan to spend a week in this lovely city to savor its nearly 400 years of history unhurriedly. Lowlanders will also need a few days to acclimate to the 7,000 foot altitude.

Traveling from west to east, you'll come to Glorieta Pass, site of a major Civil War battle in March 1862. Here a Confederate force failed in its plan to overtake New Mexico and then move northward to the Colorado gold fields.

A monument commemorates the heroics of Texas volunteers while rock formations in the background boast more recent messages: "Jesus loves you" and "Nelson loves Mark's wife"—a reminder that the present isn't far away.

Indian Pueblo ruins, which date back to 1450, lie only a couple miles from town. We descended into the underground gloom of a kiva—a ceremonial chamber—and began to imagine the earlier inhabitants engaged in religious ritual. A low, steady male voice began to chant, and the eerie sound echoed around the circular walls of the tiny sanctum, lending even greater realism. We saw the elders sitting trance-like on the hard-packed floor, their wrinkled faces expressionless as they related tribal history to the young men before them.

Knowledge of one's people, of belonging, of continuity of time—all these elements of the human experience were transferred from generation to generation in this room. And they were the same reasons behind *our* presence on the trail.

Historic Jackpot

Cycling on, we discovered an old highway parallels the interstate into the town of Las Vegas, which claims to be the meeting place of the mountains and the plains. The time of year and altitude variances did indeed provide us with spectacular views—black Angus cows on bright green valley grass, rich fall colors along the mesas, white-topped mountains to the northwest and, as advertised, the beginnings of the almost endless auburn plains. We visited the "Rough Rider's Museum" in town, and saw a Steinway piano which had bounced its way to Santa Fe in a Conestoga wagon. Next to it were gleaming swords used by some of Teddy Roosevelt's local volunteers in the Spanish-American War.

But by far the most interesting part of the town were the museum caretakers, a Mrs. Crabtree and Mr. Thatcher, who were full of lore about the trail. A 30-minute visit became a three-hour stay.

Thirty miles northeast of Las Vegas is the Fort Union National Monument—a well-preserved 1851 army fort built to protect the Santa Fe travelers from Kiowa and Comanche attack. It was dusk as we returned from the site, and the memory of a brilliant sunset giving such color to the trail ruts which paralleled our road remains with me as one of the most exquisite moments of the ride. The knowledge of what history lay behind those luminescent earthen scars transported us to another age. Had the sun retired that evening and dawned the following day on a world of horses and covered wagons, I think we would not have been so surprised, nor so very unhappy.

The Indians Defend

We saw many prairie graves on our ride. Some pioneers were probably felled by disease and others by warring bands of Indians. We passed one spot where in 1850, ten heavily-armed men crouched behind their dead horses during a harrowing day-long battle with the Apache and Ute Indians. They were finally overcome, and massacred.

The Trail Divides

When the cyclist reaches the little town of Springer—130 miles from Santa Fe—he or she must choose between the northern and southern routes of the trail. As shown by the map, the northern "mountain" path continues over the now-easy Raton Pass into Colorado, then eastward into Kansas. This was the arduous original route of "Father of the Trail" Becknell in 1821. The southern loop heads east on US 56 to Clayton, glances off the Texas state border, then crosses the Oklahoma panhandle to the town of Cimarron. This little Kansas village takes its name from wagon trains heading to Santa Fe who branched south across 60-odd miles of arid desert, leaving the waters of the Arkansas, and praying that the Cimarron River would appear before the mules and horses died. The route was called the Cimarron Cutoff, but was also referred to as the Jornada—short for Jornada de la Muerte, or Journey of Death.

And so it almost was for Becknell when in 1822, on his second trip to Santa Fe, he decided to avoid the time-consuming Raton Pass of the mountain route. His small party ran dry; the mules' ears were cut off in hopes that the hot blood would quench the men's thirst. When the end was near, a buffalo happened by. He was quickly shot and carefully gutted—for the water carried in his distended stomach gave Becknell and his men strength to push on. Years later one man who had been present that day declared "nothing every passed his lips which gave him such exquisite delight as his first draught of that filthy beverage."

The decision of which route to take is not easy. Head north and you will glimpse the high Rockies in the distance, and visit a completely reconstructed Bent's Old Fort—named for the brothers who built it in 1834. We spent a long afternoon with the fort personnel, climbed the parapets to look across the Arkansas River at land which once was Mexico, and marvelled at the huge B-52's that fly past this piece of history toward their nearby base.

If you choose the Jornada—the southern branch—you'll take in lovely desert scenes, as well as trail landmarks of Round Mound and Point of Rocks. Rest assured that you'll not have to begin nibbling on your handlebars halfway through this route, for small towns exist at manageable intervals.

Legendary Dodge City

Whichever route you choose, you'll ride through Dodge City, Kansas—a town at its best during a time when "there was no civilization west of St. Louis, and no God west of Dodge." The graves at Boot Hill are vivid proof—consider one Jack Reynolds, who died in 1872. His tombstone reads, "A notoriously mean and contemptible desperado who was forever quitted at Dodge city by a track-layer, who put six balls through him before he could say Scat!" Not all the graves belonged to cowboys, however. Alice Chambers, who died in 1878, was a full-fledged member of the group referred to as "soiled doves." A "favorite of many," her last words were: "Circumstances led me to this end."

Dodge City, Fort Larned, and Pawnee Rock, the Caches and Council Grove, all these towns and landmarks filled with Santa Fe Trail history will pop into life as you pedal by—and they'll never quite fade away. Nor will the people—those who live along the route today, whose eyes light up when you tell them why you're riding the trail. They may well fill an afternoon telling stories of their ancestors.

I won't forget the 60-year-old woman who appeared out of nowhere as we entered Colorado. Riding a bright yellow motorbike, she regaled us with stories of eastern Colorado history. She also knew the marsh hawks and other birds which flew up on occasion. And we missed her company when she turned to putter back to town.

The subdued winter colors of Colorado and Kansas were lovely, but the final miles into my home state of Missouri, past Arrow Rock and into Franklin were the trail had begun, were especially sweet to me. All the travelers of a century before had come to life through their written words, and the relived trail. Of course, we had it easier—paved roads and an occasional motel. But just like those who went before, I now know of Kansas winds, and prairie chills, and the mournful sounds of coyotes far off on a still night.